Live in the
REAL!

REAL is Rare.
Let's Make it Normal.

ARK SARDAROV

Live in the REAL!
REAL is Rare. Let's Make it Normal.
©2024, Ark Sardarov

ISBN 979-8-35094-917-9
ISBN eBook: 979-8-35094-918-6

REAL is Rare. Let's Make it Normal.

Face the elephant in *your* room and Live in the REAL! Unbury the truths in your life to finally live your genuine and authentic self. Untangle and free yourself from today's age of social disconnection, digital miscommunication, and societal false paradigms. Transform your existence into a REAL life of depth and meaning. This is the straight-forward, clear, and simple approach to life, known as the pragmatic philosophy of *REALogy*®.

Let's Get One Thing Straight....

This is not a *motivational* self-improvement book. I'm not here to motivate you in the short-term. I'm here to inspire you for the rest of your life. This is not a "rah-rah", "you can do it", "just think positive" push. This is a DNA-penetrating, soul-activating, *inspirational and inspiring* endeavor that will force you to become your own perpetual and inherent self-motivating individual. It will empower you, by extracting the power that already resides in you, to be unburied, harnessed and forever embraced. Your sense of existence as your true self will always feel heightened because living in the immediate moment will become the base template of your life.

The word "motivation" typically calls for a third-party stimulant to serve as a motivating trigger of some type. In other words, you are reliant on someone else/thing to motivate you to action or thought. Although effective in the short-term (and sometimes in the long-term), this method is typically short-lived and fleeting, causing you to tire of that trigger and ultimately lose desire to continue. I prefer the word "inspiration" because once you are intrinsically inspired, it stays with you for the long-term. You don't have to rely on a stimulating trigger any longer to motivate you. You are self-motivated because the initial inspiration is still ingrained in you. I'm here to "teach you how to fish" for your ultimate and permanent transcendent growth, not simply hand you the "fish" as your meal of temporary survival.

This is a life-awakening inspirational platform in which *YOU* are intrinsically and permanently inspired to find your true REAL self and identity. Motivation is a misnomer. It is temporary, ethereal, and sometimes misguided. Once you are permanently inspired to be the person you are meant to be, motivation becomes unnecessary. Because inspiration is an inward choice you make, it easily becomes a permanent fixture in your life. Inspiration *IS* the essence of self-help, at its core. Being inspired ignites self-help into action.

My goal is to launch you and guide you to finding yourself, your purpose, and the meanings in your life (yes, meanings—there are many). You will forever change the way you think about yourself, your loved ones, your career, your mind, your life, and the greater lives of humanity. A major paradigm shift in your soul, comprised of your mind, psyche, heart, and spirit, will inspire you to understand your purpose and passions. Not only will you unearth, re-define, and re-wire your authentic self since your own birth, but you will comprehensively understand who you are and how you got here since the birth of humanity itself. Through this self-inspiration, you will forever live in a default and subliminal state of tapped-in self-mo-tivation, without having to rely on anyone but yourself.

In fact, after reading this book, my goal is for you to forget who I am and move forward in your life with the newly hard-wired inspi-rational tools of your life. Yes, my goal is to ultimately lose my readers because they simply don't need me anymore. I don't want to be your motivator. I want to be your life *Inspirer*. Come take this journey with me. Real is rare. Let's make it normal together.

What is REALogy®?

REALogy® is my creation of a pragmatic philosophy in which truth undeniably penetrates your life and merges with your DNA to uncover your REAL, authentic self, one that is living in the real. Living in the REAL is living in the truth, every minute, every hour, and every day of your life, without equivocation. It forms a clear and straight-forward sense of direction in life.

"It is our duty to improve ourselves."

IMMANUEL KANT

A *REAL* Footnote

Because the goal of this endeavor is to permanently inspire you to be the ultimate version of your true self, I've addressed the most important aspects and areas in the life of the present-day human being. I realize that each and every chapter of this book can be a voluminous book of its own. The human being is a vastly complex animal, as we know. However, I've attempted to dive deep into the most critical and self-revealing meanings of our lives to unearth the inherent inspiration that resides in you. I've created what I call STAGES of your life, which cover these areas in the most blatantly truthful way possible, culminating in The Final Blast-Off Stage, in which you come to life as your true self and start living in *REALogy®*. This book need not be read in the order that I've created since you may be inclined to focus on the more important Stages sooner than my order suggests. My order of these Stages is not by importance, it is simply what I believe to be the most logical order of progression of the arrival to your true self. Enjoy!

"It's better to be a person for a day than
to be a shadow for 1,000 days."

BUDDHIST PROVERB

TABLE OF TRUTHS

STAGE 0: Your Life is Precious (Life is *Not* Hard) 1

STAGE 1: Living (and Sleeping) in the Bed of Truth 13

STAGE 2: Time is Our Priceless Commodity 27

STAGE 3: Change is the Constant Currency 33

STAGE 4: The Power of Your Mind 39

STAGE 5: Transcend Your Personal History 55

STAGE 6: Total Health & Fitness
(The Ultimate Key to Longevity and Prolonged Life) 63

STAGE 7: Total Life Fitness (Daily Life Enhancement Goals) 83

STAGE 8: Your Human Relationships 91

STAGE 9: The False Identity Crisis (The Career Identity Fallacy) 111

STAGE 10: Your Relationships with Money, Materialism,
Addictions, and Social Media 119

STAGE 11: Live from Love Not Fear
(Destroy Your Survival-Based Default) 131

STAGE 12: The Meanings of Life and Human Existence 139

STAGE 13: The Undeniable Belief in the Power of Miracles
(The Reasons Why Things Happen to You) 149

STAGE 14: Men and Women are More Alike than They are Different. 155

STAGE 15: REAL, Effective, and Efficient Communication
(Words are Everything)..169

STAGE 16: Your Personal Growth 183

STAGE 17: The REAL You vs. The Real World (A Daily Dilemma)..... 195

STAGE 18: Faith, Spirituality, and Religion...203

FINAL STAGE 19: BLAST OFF!!!: You've Come to Life!....................217

Bullet Summaries of the Major Concluding Themes:..........................221

STAGE 0:

Your Life is Precious
(Life is *Not* Hard)

Stage Zero is the ground zero of life. Therefore, we have to start at zero, the origin of life, do we not? I think most of us have said at one time, "life is precious." Most often however, we use this term after a tragic event that reminds us of the preciousness of our lives. Then we typically forget and move on with our lives.

These three important words should never be forgotten. We must always understand and value the very basic and primary tenet of human existence, in that, life is precious, short, and never guaranteed. This must be ingrained in our core so that it's always front of mind, so that we don't even have to be reminded of it, it's just always there. When you live your life and operate with this understanding as part of your DNA and identity, your awareness of yourself and your life is now viewed from a completely authentic perspective.

Let's dive deeper. What is life? It is essentially three major facets. It is your specific life that you're living. It is also your specific physical body that is biologically living this life. And lastly, it is the broader concept of life that includes all of humanity and the meanings within it.

Let's start with your life. You need to really accept and truly understand that you only have one life, right? At least that we know of. If we understand this notion conceptually, why do so many of us "waste" our lives by not living our fullest potential? We say that life is a miracle. Well, it truly is. Birth is a miracle and life is a miracle. So even when we know and acknowledge that life itself is a miracle and not guaranteed, we still tend to take our lives for granted and arrogantly believe that we have plenty of "time" in the future. Future? That's crazy. We inherently know that the future is not guaranteed. You have to live your life now!

As I write this, none of us, I mean NONE of us, is guaranteed one more precious second of life, let alone the next day, month, or year. There are 86,400 seconds in one day and not one of them is guaranteed to us. Why are we so arrogant to think that we will wake up tomorrow, that a terminal illness won't take us down, that a fatal accident won't happen, that a terrorist threat doesn't upend our lives, or literally one of a million other scenarios that proves the no-guarantee fact of life? Even worse than not living to our potential, some of us are trapped behind masks of other lives or buried under insidious addictions from which we cannot un-trap ourselves. Wake up and simply understand and internalize that your life is precious. Your life is short. It is not guaranteed. Start there, at the very basic level. Hold these thoughts dear to you every single day of your life.

When you really live from this understanding, not only do you value your life on a daily basis, but you actually start caring more for other peoples' lives too. Other people naturally become more important to you, particularly your loved ones, because you want to make sure you exist in their lives for as long as humanly possible.

This way of living morphs into a positive Catch-22 where you start to value your life so much more, simply because you value of the lives of others. Isn't that how it should be? Isn't that a bit more refreshing?

If we doggedly and undeniably believe that life is precious, short, and never guaranteed, not only do we value our life more, but now we start to realize that our physical body is also of paramount importance, right? Because without our biological body, we have no life. We need our body to live our life. I cannot make it simpler than that. Then why do so many of us not take care of our bodies and our health the way we should? It's simply because we haven't accepted and ingrained into our core the extreme value of our life and our physical body.

Our best version of a life lived long and healthy starts with our physical well-being. The older we get, the more important it becomes to live a healthy lifestyle well into our older years. Ironically however, most people don't realize this until their older years when their bodies start breaking down. This awareness needs to come to fruition much earlier in life to create a preventative mindset, and clearly the younger the better.

We'll delve further into the specific details of health and fitness in Stage Six, but for now, the most important and simplest concept to understand, to start you on the right path of permanent health, is the following. Any and every single time we literally raise our hand to our mouth to place an item of food or beverage in it, we must be actively, intently, and purposely aware of exactly the item we are about to eat and ingest. The minute we swallow that item, there is no going back. That's it. We can never live that same moment again. Think about that. For that moment, and possibly for the long term, we may have negatively affected our health if that item was not supposed to go in our mouth. Knowing that, why would we ever want to do such a thing? We only think of our mouths as the mechanism to eat and enjoy our meals. We also need to start thinking of it as the gateway of permanent ingestion of every substance that goes inside of it. And I haven't even mentioned the illicit drugs (and even some prescription drugs) that we purposely ingest and/or inject into our body. I'm merely talking about the unhealthy lifestyle of eating and drinking.

We have to literally cherish our body by viewing our mouths as the permanent and discriminating gatekeeper of a healthy body, not an open portal to everyone and everything. We have to remember that we only have one physical body. There's no replacing it. The younger we are when we fully accept and live by this understanding, the longer our healthy life will be. Whoever created the human body, has built the most amazing and perfect specimen. The human body is made in such a glorious way. Every cell, tissue, and organ work in the most perfect unison and relentless synchronicity to consistently and effortlessly provide sustained life for you every millisecond of your existence. Your heart literally never stops, it never takes a beat off. It performs endlessly and tirelessly. It has to.

The best part is that even when you do negative things to your body (eating bad food, drinking alcohol, taking drugs), your body will ALWAYS try to recover, and will recover. It is in a permanent state of homeostasis, wherein, it always tries to mend itself and come back to the mean of good health. It keeps doing this over and over again, no matter how often and how much you choose to "damage" it. It will unconditionally do this for you for quite a while. Until it won't anymore. The moment the point of no return is triggered, your loyal body won't be able to recover, even though it wants to and tries. Your body not only has a natural healthy shelf life of a maximum of 100 to 120 years, but that shelf life is reduced by the amount and the rate of "damage" done to it. It is a machine of incredible wonder, but it also has its physical limitations.

The simple takeaway is — do not do it. Don't continue to damage your body until it is unable to unconditionally and un-judgmentally recover for you. Easier said than done, right? Yes, that's true. But if you start to live this way at a young age or simply make the commitment to at any change, then it's not a problem. It becomes your permanent healthy lifestyle. But if you're stuck in a negative mode of maligning your body, particularly if it's an insidious addiction of some type, it is much more difficult to change course, and even feels impossible. But it's very doable. It starts with your unequivocal understanding and appreciation of your life and your body. This will lead to your committed desire to change and/or accept third-party intervention to help you effect that change.

For example, if you were to see someone collapse in front you, you would immediately call for help and start rendering aid to that person. No question about it. You wouldn't think twice about helping a fellow human in need. Then why don't you do that for your own life now? View yourself as someone in need, without judging yourself for it. Do not wait for the most obvious scenario of you collapsing at some point. Think of your body as if it's in a slow state of collapse now, so long as you're not taking care of it. Your body needs that aid now! Just because your body hasn't collapsed yet and you aren't consciously aware of the negative internal accumulations leading to the breaking point, it doesn't mean that you're fine. Quite the contrary; you are simply a slowly ticking time bomb of a significant physical catastrophe. Do not wait until a future when it might be too late. The aid that is needed now is so easy and simple. It doesn't require calling 911 or anyone else. All it requires is your own commitment to start taking care of your body. That's it.

Let me offer another more visually repulsive example. If I were to ask you to pick up the corpse of a dead rat and take a bite of it, you would cringe and convulse at the mere thought of it, let alone waste a second actually thinking about doing such a thing. Then why would you *knowingly* ingest the permanent toxins of unhealthy foods, excessive alcohol consumption, cigarettes, or illicit drugs? Why would you knowingly do such a crazy and obviously detrimental thing to your body? You would not, right? But sadly, people do. Many still smoke, consume unhealthy portions of alcohol, ingest illicit drugs, in addition to their unhealthy eating habits. That's the horribly ingrained thought process that we must alter.

We have to understand the simple fact that literally anything and everything YOU choose to put in your mouth or into your body (by other means), that you have now taken ownership of whether that item is going to help your body or hurt your body. You have the choice, and certainly the power to make that choice. No one has a gun to your head telling you to take a bite of a dead rat. When you change your narrative in your mind, you change your life. Jesse Jackson once said that you can only control the dash on your tombstone between the date you were born and the date you died, not the dates on either side of that dash. I will add that the more in control you are of that dash, the later you can push off the date to the right of that dash. Grasp the power of this choice. It is 100% yours.

We have established that your life and your body are forever sacred from the minute you are born. More importantly, your default psyche knows this to be true. Now that you're ready and have begun to live your life in a much more purposeful way where you value every moment you have on this Earth, understanding the larger picture of life becomes much clearer. Your eyes open up and receive the beauty of life and humanity. You begin to see the many meanings of life and significantly appreciate the lives of others beyond yourself and immediate loved ones. (Stage 12 will cover the meanings of life in more detail.) You gain a broader thirst for knowledge and ultimately wisdom. You realize that wisdom goes far beyond just knowledge, that knowledge simply prepares you for a game show, but wisdom prepares you for the ultimate game of life.

You have an epiphany! It's so clear now. You realize that when people utter the over-used cliché of "life is hard", that this notion is completely wrong. It makes no sense anymore. It's a copout; it's false and completely misleading. Life is not hard. As Confucius said, "Life is really simple, but we insist on making it more complicated." So true.

Beyond that, we make it more complicated because we do not know how to face the unexpected challenges. Even worse, we're in denial of these challenges and pretend they don't exist. As we lie to ourselves every day, living life becomes more challenging every day. Life is actually very simple, and should be made simple. We all have challenges, adversities, and tragedies in our lives, some are much more debilitating than others. But the key is to take every single one of those seriously from the very beginning. You have to see the true nature of the challenge for what it is in order to understand it fully. Once you see it from a perspective of truth, the next step of resolving this challenge and moving on with your life, is more often than not, an obvious solution. The "life is hard" part only comes in to play the minute you don't acknowledge the challenge and begin a process of denial. Now the cycle of oppression by this challenge onto your life has begun. Once that happens, particularly on a repeated basis, you become overwhelmed, frustrated, and defeated. You feel like there's no hope. But there is. It always starts with baby steps. Being in the moment is the first step, and taking one step in front of the other is the next step. Taking pride in your power to take control of your life now begins to build into a consistent level of internal confidence, which turns into a viable hope that is pervasive in your life. You become confident and hopeful, and therefore remain on your committed path of overcoming one challenge at a time. You are seeing everything clearly and truthfully.

Life can get hard, however, the moment you try to take the easy choice, the short cut. Taking the harder path is what ultimately makes life easier. For example, exercising might be hard, but not moving at all makes life harder from obesity, etc. Addressing conflicts might be hard but avoiding them can create greater conflicts. Mastering your craft is hard, but having no skills makes life harder. *Easy* always has immediate costs, both actual costs and opportunity costs. But living life the right away and following the right path makes life easier by default, and more rewarding.

The next time someone says "life is hard" or "life is not fair," you will know that life is actually simple; that you can make it simple. You'll know that life IS fair because we all face various forms of unfairness. None of us is impervious to unfairness (assuming a level playing field of course). We all face obstacles and tragedies in our lives. Yes, some of us unfortunately face more challenging obstacles than others, but the minute you start feeling that way, you become trapped in an unnecessary cycle of competition wherein you're the victim. The two most important things you have to remember in this moment when this happens are (1) find reasons to be grateful (no matter how small) and (2) begin the moment-by-moment process of addressing and resolving your challenge. Be grateful of the position you are in and face your challenges head on.

When you finally and exhaustively believe in your core that (1) life is truly precious, (2) that your life and body are precious and sacred, and (3) that life is not hard because it can be made simple, you actually start feeling ALIVE in your bones every day. You can literally feel and tangibly describe what ALIVE and AWAKE feel like. You cherish every day that you wake up, you feel grateful in the experiences of your day and you actually become aware of a genuine and real feeling of being alive. You're aware of the feel of your heart pumping and your blood flowing in your veins. For the first time, you actually can palpably feel life itself and being alive in it. When you get to this point, you attain a broader awareness and understanding of your life and the lives of others. This brings you to a permanent state of self-improvement with a natural hunger to become a better person every day.

> *"Life is sacred, that is to say, it is the supreme value,*
> *to which all other values are subordinate."*
>
> ALBERT EINSTEIN

Living in the Moment

Wouldn't it be great if we could hit the pause button on life? Sometimes we need a break from life. Actually, we *can* pause life. It's called living in the moment. When you take the time to *live* in the moment, it feels like you *are* pausing your life, and thereby reveling in the moment. You know the feeling you have when you get lost listening to one of your favorite songs? In that moment, everything else in your world has suddenly disappeared, except for the song you're lost in. When you snap out of it, you realize you're back in the world again. That was precisely an exact instance of living in the moment and not realizing it, a moment that was involuntarily created for you and manifested by a song.

You can actually create these moments for yourself. When you synchronize your mind and body to literally feel and absorb every second of a moment you're experiencing, it feels like a real, momentary pause that is then filled with clarity, understanding, and awareness. It is an incredible feeling, one that you'll want to re-create. To truly live in the moment, do the following to the best of your ability.

a. Remove from your mind all your surrounding distractions. Even if you can't control certain distractions in the area you're in, you have to force your mind and thoughts to ignore and remove them to the best of your ability.

b.   Remind yourself that the past is done, it's irrelevant. The future is unknown. Therefore, all you have and all you know is the present.

c.   Slow down your breathing, almost to the point of meditation.

d.   Practice mindfulness.

e.   Tap into your mind, thoughts, and body to synchronize them as one.

f.   Feel, absorb, and enjoy literally every second of the moment you're experiencing.

g.   Allow new and free thoughts of clarity to enter your mind as you're living in the moment.

h.   Feel the joy and contentment of the moment.

All you can really know is the *now*, right? Ultimately, the moment you are in is all we know. The past is behind and the future isn't guaranteed, so we have to know the now, and more importantly, we have to *believe* in the now. The now is all we know for certain, in that moment. While planning and making goals for the future is good, and should be done, thinking that you are guaranteed and entitled to a future is not the perspective you should hold. Since the next moment is never guaranteed, life can be taken almost instantly.

Many people live for the future, meaning that (1) they think there is time for the future to arrive or that time allows for the future to happen in its natural course and (2) they make precision planning of their lives for the future, meaning they are relying on future results to materialize. Again, you must set goals for the future, but with a full awareness and appreciation of living in the moment. The present is the only precious asset you have. You have to intentionally live and appreciate every moment. Death is sadly the ultimate equalizer for us all...*memento mori.* It does not discriminate in favor of any person or in favor of any planned and pending result in the future. The absolute belief in the now and the genuine understanding and appreciation of all its requisite meanings is a crux of life, one of many to be addressed.

STAGE 1:

Living (and Sleeping) in the Bed of Truth

Truth is easy. It is simple—it is real and completely involuntary in nature. You never have to think about speaking the truth. It just happens; it pours out of you, as it should. A lie, on the other hand, you have to create it and think of it before you speak. Now if you really think about it, well beyond the life you've come to know, how silly is it that the concept of lying even exists in human nature? How wrong is it that someone can actually lie to you, or vice versa? Doesn't that very thought on a deeper level trouble you?

There is no reason for humans to lie. Unfortunately, humans created rationalized reasons to lie because they decided that the short-term perceived benefits of lying outweighed the realities of truth. Consequently, lying became a normal part of life for all humans to the point where it's hardly questioned any more. The fact that I'm posing this question shocks you a bit because lying is a deep-rooted fact of civilized societies that goes unquestioned. Most of us don't think of ourselves as liars because we've rationalized in our own minds that we're not liars, even though we are deep down, at least to some extent.

When living in the truth every day, your life becomes the purest—genuine and simple. What do I mean by that? Truth, and living with it, has to encompass every aspect of your life. I'm not only talking about being honest, although that's obviously important and part of it as well. I am talking about seeing the truth and the REAL in every situation. More importantly, having the ability to see it clearly without being influenced by your urge to ignore it or your sense of denial is the approach.

Truth is difficult to define, but you know it when you see it, right? The very second you see truth, you know it's true. Even if you're not quite sure, your inner voice of truth speaks to you. In that moment, you will either accept it, or you will defy it. It's your choice to make in that moment. It happens so quickly, often times, that most people are not consciously aware that they've made a choice. If you deny the truth, it's easy for your mind to rationalize that it wasn't a choice. If that truth scares you, goes against your prior thought process, or reveals something about yourself you want to stay hidden, your default reaction will be to defy it and deny it. When you do that, you are now lying to yourself and living in a state of denial and defensiveness.

Imagine for a moment a modern-day world where the concept of "denial" doesn't exist, where lying doesn't even occur and where everyone literally speaks the truth every time. Pretend that the words "lie", "deceit", "denial" and all their respective synonyms are not in the dictionary, that they never were. And that they don't exist in any other language in the world. Wouldn't that notion alone make the world an amazing and beautiful place? Mankind would naturally and automatically care for each other more. Hatred would not exist.

Most of the ills of the world would not exist. People would approach each other with love and acceptance instead of fear and hatred. Is it impossible for such a world to exist? Would you be surprised if I told you it already exists and we're just blind to it?

If the world were to be run by children, we would have this world of truth that I'm describing. Such a world already exists for children. The minute we are born, we don't know lying and deceit. We are born in truth, not as liars. We are born with not even an inkling of the concept of lying. It doesn't exist in children. Children are the most honest humans we know. As they grow, they live their lives in the truth every day. Unfortunately however, there is a limit, one that was created by the world we live in. Once they're introduced to lying (typically by adults' poor modeling) or accidentally become aware of it, they start to lie, initially as a test. They don't stop lying because they become aware of the fact that everyone lies around them and that it appears to be the norm. And sadly, they're not taught *not* to lie. After all, children learn from and model after the adults in their lives. This norm is further perpetuated by parents and other adults who do not strongly enforce and teach their children that lying is wrong. Sadly, they give up on this most crucial teaching moment of a child's life when a child is the most prone to learning.

Humanity, from the very beginning, has incorporated lying in its daily interaction with one another. Why is that the case? Why is that the norm, albeit an accepted norm? We all know that lying is wrong, so why is it so pervasive in our every dialogue, communication, and exchange? Lying in court is a crime, with a fancy name of perjury. Why isn't lying in life a crime, or at least forbidden? We must ask ourselves these important questions. We must delve deep for the answers and be honest about the discussion.

The human species is the only one in the animal kingdom that uses rational thought to create an untruth. Because we have the ability to think on a critical level, humans have chosen to create the concept of lying. All other animals, outside of humans, live in their most genuine state, in which they are not in denial about who they are. They operate on both instinct and rational thought, but they do not deny who they really are to themselves; they're not able. Animals are always living in the moment and they accept themselves for who they are, undeniably. They don't live with false identities of themselves. They live in their most natural and purest state, free of lying, one moment to the next. Humans can do this too, but we have simply chosen not to. Why do we allow rational thought to deny who we really are? And why do some of us do so to such an extent that we are living lives behind masks, never in touch with our true selves and true identities as a result?

Frank Kafka said it perfectly when he was quoted, "I was ashamed of myself when I realized life is a costume party and I attended with my real face." Many people unfortunately wear masks once they've buried their inner truths in permanent graves by their lies. The truth doesn't care however. That's the beauty of truth. It doesn't care what you do with it. Every lie incurs a debt to the truth. Sooner or later that debt will be paid. And you don't get to pick when you can speak the truth again, once you're on the insidious path of lying. Not until you have completely come clean, made full amends, and asked for forgiveness. Even then, the truth doesn't see you the same anymore.

Why is it that children and animals are able to live in the truth every moment of their lives without any denial or equivocation about who they are, but we do not? What's worse is that we've *chosen* to live such a life. We did this to ourselves, this unfathomable, vicious cycle of denial. We may have forgotten or not ever realized when that choice was made, but it was certainly made at some point, which then altered the course of the rest of our lives. It's sad when you think of it in those real terms. Truth is the shortest distance from point A to

B; it's always the most direct route. A lie has no end point; it is the beginning of a long and meandering road with no navigation or GPS available. One gets so lost in it that the starting point disappears in the rear view mirror.

The great news is that truth is within our grasp and our complete control. While we cannot change the way society functions and how people treat you, we can certainly choose to control how we live our lives going forward. That choice is to live in the truth, every moment and every day, with genuine effort and intent. People will let us down. In virtually every area where there is human life, we will be let down by our friends, our family, our colleagues, elected officials, our governments, etc. Despite all this, we still have complete control of how we choose to live our lives. No one can take that away from us.

You know how when we've had a few drinks of alcohol, our guard drops a bit, and sprinkles of truth start exuding from our pores, our mouth, and our behavior? These are the truths that are waiting to come out when you're not strong enough to allow them in a sober state of rational thought. Our body language always speaks the truth. Our bodies haven't perfected the correct synchronization with our minds when we're telling a lie. The body always indicates otherwise when the spoken word is a lie. Crying is another example of truth from body language. When you cry involuntarily, especially if you didn't see it coming, you are living in the truth at that very moment. Isn't that how babies communicate their truth of their moment to us? You have to listen to these truths and you have to be brave enough to take the necessary control of your life to start making changes from the truths revealed to you.

There is another important perspective of truth that serves as a constant reminder that it is ever-present in our lives. Art is truth. Art is borne of and resides in truth, since the beginning of time. Every single representation of art in human form, such as music, books, paintings, plays, movies, comedians, architecture, sculptures, comedy, tragedy, etc., has its origins in truth. Art does not lie. It exists to exemplify, amplify and expose the truth. Even when art has an ironic twist of a lie in it, that lie's only purpose is to bravely expose the truth of the matter. Every artist conveys a snapshot of truth in life as a permanent living representation of truth. In fact, since the beginning of time, artists have been persecuted, vilified and killed for exposing some of our deeper, unbearable truths.

As the audience members for all of these forms of art, we live for art. We love it, we enjoy and we long for it. Many of us rely on it for our very survival. I know I do. However, isn't it incredibly ironic that our daily human behavior and interaction with each other doesn't reconcile with the truth symbolized in our art? We love and enjoy the representation of truth in art, yet we do not live and abide by this same truth for which we just displayed our appreciation. A bit hypocritical, isn't it? In fact, the main reason why we find enjoyment in art is that it speaks to the hidden truth inside of us with which we're afraid to live. It directly speaks to our creative soul that correlates to the truthful creation by the artist.

We all have a creative side. We psychologically and subliminally long to feel the embrace of this truth in the form of our chosen art that speaks to us. This is a reassuring sign and clear indication that there is a big part of us that wants to somehow be able to unearth our truth within us and find a way to live with it in peace. This is precisely why we purchase various works of art. To that endeavor, I urge you to pursue that spark of your desire to unbury your truths to start making the necessary changes in your life. If you are able to see the truth in the art which you've chosen to enjoy, then you will be able to un-trap your truths that are buried in you.

Living with truth in your life is such a pure and simple way of living. It is refreshing, it is uplifting. It is intrinsic and it ultimately reveals who you really are once you make it your default setting in your mind, psyche, heart, and spirit, all of which define your soul. It becomes normal, involuntary, and amazingly easy. You're truly free as a result and experience ultimate freedom. There's no second guessing, no pausing, no paralysis by analysis. It guides you in the right direction all the time. It makes living life easy. Most importantly, you become permanently in touch with your true identity and thus conduct yourself with this identity 100% of the time without denial and equivocation. Your outlook and perspective are always positive and self-inspiring. This daily, permanent lifestyle, in turn, reduces (if not eliminates) stress and illnesses, makes you healthier, prolongs your life, and improves your quality of life. As we know, stress alone is one of the greatest causes of illnesses, some terminal.

The easiest way to change your life to living one of truth is to remember how you were as a young child before the ways of society grabbed a hold of you. Remember how you used to laugh constantly, play and run around incessantly, and most importantly, how you were living your authentic self? You didn't know otherwise or anything but your authentic self. Start at that childhood stage and re-engineer your life little by little. Start exposing the truths in your life to yourself of the things you've been hiding from or in denial. Try to laugh more, especially when you feel the pain of a difficult truth you just exposed. Laughter will help you face it and get through it.

Expose everything about yourself to yourself. Break yourself down and start new, like a newborn. Once you start the re-building process, you need to be aware of and avoid the pitfalls of deceit and denial. Be intently and consciously aware of every choice you're making, particularly the small ones. The small details make up the whole of who you are. They all have to align together for you to be your authentic self. And if you ever have any doubts, take a pause and listen to your inner voice. That inner voice always speaks the truth. It will always steer you in the right direction.

Once you hard wire your mind to consistently see the truth without equivocation on a consistent basis, you can now apply it in practical terms to every aspect of your life on a daily basis. For example, you can start asking yourself the following questions within the key areas of your life.

a.   *Health* — Am I truly taking care of myself? Am I eating healthy, staying consistently active and getting enough sleep every night? Am I avoiding an extreme lifestyle of erratic behavior and endeavors? Do I take the time to focus on my well-being and longevity? Do I love myself enough to stay on top of my health.

b.   *Career* — Am I doing what I love, or at least have some level of passion and/or enjoyment in my job? Am I anxious about going to work or am I at least happy to go to work every day? Do I enjoy my work environment? Do I go through the motions without putting in additional effort? Does my job feel like a grind, or am I enjoying it so much that I forget I'm working?

c.   *Romantic Relationship* — Am I happy with my partner? Are we truly compatible? Do I enjoy being with my partner? Are we communicating on deeper levels and actually listening to one another? Is this my lifelong partner? Are we both friends and lovers in our relationship? If you're single and/or dating, am I content with my current situation? Do I not want to be in a relationship? Am I in one because of pressure? It's important to understand that it's perfectly okay to not to want to be in a relationship.

d.   *Family Relationship* — If I'm in a committed relationship and/ or with kids, am I truly connected to my partner and/or my children? Am I actively involved in all the lives of my partner and children? Do I focus on quality time together? Do I remind myself that family always comes first no matter what? If single with no kids, do I stay connected and in contact with my parent(s) and siblings? Do I participate in all family functions? Do I see my parent(s) and siblings often enough without any reason? Do I appreciate what my family members do for me on a regular basis (including spouse, parents, children and siblings)? Do I take them for granted? Do I verbalize the appreciation and give thanks?

These are just some of the hard-hitting questions you have to ask yourself. You have to take the time and ask yourself these questions on a regular basis. Periodic self-reflection, self-evaluation, and self-awareness are key components of reminding yourself of the truths in your life and if you are living up to them. This consistent practice will prevent you from living a life filled with denials and false truths.

You literally have to look at yourself in the mirror, stare into your own eyes so hard that you penetrate your own soul, and ask yourself these questions. While maintaining strict focus on your eyes, you have to answer yourself with complete 100% honestly. If you lie, you'll see your eyes flinching. There's no point in lying to yourself now that you've come to a place of exposing your truths. This is very difficult work, but it becomes easier over time once you've made this consistent practice the norm. Ultimately, you will come to a place in your life where seeing the truth is so easy, instant, and clear, that you'll become a master at instantly spotting the lies. This will become involuntary. You will see the truths clearly, and you will spot the lies instantly. You will become a master lie detector.

Let me offer another complementary approach to consistently living a life in a bed of truth. Using myself as an example, I was very fortunate at a young age to learn and master the following principle: once you know something, you can NEVER *un-know* it. In other words, once you learn and accept something to be true, from that point forward, if you live your life in violation of that truth, then you're lying to yourself. Once your brain learns and comes to know something new, you can never trick your brain into thinking that you never learned it. Your brain is too smart for that. There is no delete button, there is no reset button. Your brain holds you accountable to that new found knowledge, to the truth of the matter. When you try to un-know something, it's called rationalizing and equivocating. It's called lying to yourself, which starts the vicious cycle of being in denial.

Once you learn something to be true, you should absorb it as the truth and live your life accordingly with that new awareness. I was somehow able to figure this out at a young age in my teens. I honestly began living my life accordingly. For example, if you're a smoker, you're clearly aware in this day and age how smoking is an incredibly unhealthy habit that is shortening your life, right? But have you stopped? No. Why? You know the truth about smoking, a truth that you can NEVER un-know, yet you choose to live in contradiction of that truth. If you can never un-know a truth that you've learned to be true, why would you ever live in opposition of it? It makes no sense, right?

By not deviating from truth, I was able to stay away from all the bad and negative aspects of life with this basic approach to my life. For example, I saw at a young age in my family how smoking and drinking were very unhealthy habits. Every single family member of mine was a smoker and drinker. In that moment of realization at a young age, I simply decided I would never smoke or drink. I broke the cycle in my family. I literally have never smoked in my life and am a very light social drinker (sometimes I go months without a single drink). Similarly, I grew up during the age of Nancy Reagan preaching "Say no to drugs!" So, I did. I said no to drugs because I learned the truth that they were bad. I've never tried any type of illicit drug, including marijuana. I've been completely clean my entire life — free of smoking, drinking, and drug use. I'm extremely thankful and proud of that.

I also learned at a very young age (at seventeen) that health and fitness are crucial to a long and physically prosperous life. I was fortunate enough at a young age to be exposed to a gym environment, in which, I would go to the gym on a daily basis to stay healthy and fit. I have literally never stopped since the age of seventeen. Why would I? I can honestly say that there has never been more than a couple of days (perhaps a week max on vacation) that I've never not hit the gym for my routine workout. Getting married and having kids did not stop me from going to the gym and staying fit, as it typically does to most people. When they're young and single, they stay in shape. When they marry, most fall out of that mindset. Why? It makes no sense. The minute I incorporated health and fitness in my life, it became permanent. There was no other option for me; anything otherwise would be living a life with a lie.

Can you imagine if there was a law that said you had to go to the gym at least X number of times per week to maintain your health and fitness? It would be an actual crime if you didn't, one for which you could be prosecuted. Why isn't there one? I'm being facetious of course. But in a way, it's not that bad of an idea. This is an extreme example of the way my mind works once truth has entered it. I feel like a criminal if I don't live by my own truths. For me, I truly feel like I'm lying to myself and violating my truths if I don't follow them. Every time I learn something new to be true, I accept it in my mind and tell myself I will never deviate from that truth. Because I started living in this manner at a young age, it has become completely effortless and involuntary in my daily life. Most times I'm doing it without realizing. It's extremely rare for someone who knows me well to ask me a question like, "Hey Ark, how come you're not doing so and so anymore?" I never stop doing what I know to be true in my life.

How does your bed feel when you're trying to sleep? Do you go to sleep easily and comfortably? Do you wake up with energy, zeal, and pep? Do you wake up feeling rested, recovered, and ready to take on the new miracle of a day you are given? When you sleep in a bed of truth, the entire approach to your life is different. Your approach is supported and driven by passion, commitment, and purpose. Sleeping represents one-third of the tri-pod of life that you have to master. Proper nutrition, being physically active (i.e. working out, etc.), and getting adequate sleep are the three most important daily routines that provide for the best chance of living a long, healthy, and prosperous life. When you choose to sleep in a bed of truth, you've just made one-third of that effort easy and effortless. If your bed isn't comfortable, the bed of truth is easily within your grasp. On the journey of finding your most comfortable, restful bed, don't be afraid to go slowly, if necessary. Just be afraid of stopping. If you stop, you won't find rest in your sleep. If you keep going, sleeping every night for the rest of your life will be amazingly restful.

"…Guilty feet have got no rhythm…"

GEORGE MICHAEL

"Sometimes I can hear my bones straining under the weight of all the lives I'm not living."

JONATHAN SAFRAN FOER

The Deniability of Truth (by Ark Sardarov)

You look at me, but you don't see
You talk to me, but you're not speaking
You're hearing what I'm saying, but you're not listening
You're engaged in conversation, but there's no communication
You say you understand, but there's no empathy
You only see labels, not the soul
You only know untruths, borne from bias, not from birth.
For a child only knows Truth and none other,
Until the osmosis of ill thoughts.
Only the enlightened will of mind can break the prison of learned
untruths.
But a minority of such wills is not enough to dispel the majority.
Souls are crushed, souls are forsaken.
But I see you
I am speaking to you
I am listening to you
I am communicating with you
I understand, I empathize
I see only a soul, not a label
I hope one day you will too.
When Truth makes obsolete a lie
That is when Truth becomes undeniable.

STAGE 2:

Time is Our Priceless Commodity

How much time do we really have? The younger you are the more time you think you have. The older you are the less you think you have. But that is a simplistic, superficial perspective that doesn't really address what time really is. Time, ultimately, is the very second that you're holding in your hands in that very second. The very next second after that is not guaranteed to anyone. Not a single human being in the history of humanity has ever been guaranteed any amount of time. No such thing is possible.

The most important commodity we have is time. I don't have to tell you that. Yet again, we typically take time for granted, don't we? Most often, the seconds, hours, and days go by without us realizing it. Worse yet, they go by without us realizing and acknowledging that we can never get back that very second, hour, and day that just passed. Any and every moment that has just expired, can never be experienced again. It's just not possible. That fact alone should scare us into cherishing every moment, right? But it doesn't, because we get lost in our day-to-day cycle of perceived living without pausing to reflect on the following incredible miracle. It is a miracle that time is an equalizer that has been gifted to us, of which we all have free and equitable access. Don't let time *take* your life; *take* time and fill *it* to the brim of your life.

Time is the only commodity that cannot be valued in currency. It cannot be taken to then be sold. If millionaires and billionaires were to somehow be able to create a currency for time, they would own it outright. Perhaps then we might realize how precious time is, when we actually have to pay for it instead of it being free and abundant to us. Imagine a world where you had to pay to have time, where a currency and value were ascribed to it. Would you take it for granted then? Absolutely not. You don't take your money for granted, right? Although this wouldn't be an ideal world to live in, where time had a specific worth and value, it would certainly force us to appreciate and have the utmost respect for time and the value of time. That is the type of awareness and permanent value assessment that we should have for time. It's vital importance to our being has to be front and center.

Along with birth and death, time is the ultimate equalizer. We all have it. That's the quintessential beauty of it. You can be poverty-stricken or the richest person in the world, we all have the same time allotted to us, a mere twenty-four hours in a day. Who knows how many days each of us has? No matter who you are, you can stand toe to toe with anybody knowing that no one else has been given more time than you. Talk about life being fair. That's about as fair as you can get. We're all given the many opportunities inherent in time. Yet, we don't even have a deserved respect for time to plan on how we use it. We assume that there's plenty time left. That's the ultimate fallacy, right, the arrogance of thinking we always have plenty of time left? It's the "I'll get to it tomorrow" mentality. It's the equivalent of you taking a hundred dollar bill out of your wallet, crumpling it, and throwing it out the window.

How audacious and presumptuous of us to think and live our lives in this ill-conceived way! The younger we are the more we live that way. The older we are, the more we start to appreciate time, realizing that our minutes are starting to run short. We should be thinking this way at a very young age, not when we get old. Parents should be teaching us when we're toddlers that we have a finite amount of time on this planet. But they don't because they themselves are typically too young to have such a thought. Imagine a world where we're all taught at a young age to cherish time, taught by our parents, our schools, our public servants, our jobs, etc. I think that's the world I'd want to live in. Everything would be entirely different. The construct of our lives would be centered around planning and appreciating time, knowing that we're not guaranteed one more second of it.

Sadly in today's age, we have so many more examples than ever in our human history of how our lives can be instantly cut short without warning by indiscriminate mass shootings, terrorist attacks, unexpected terminal illnesses, terrible freak accidents, Mother Nature attacks, wars, and violent conflicts, etc. This list is literally endless. We have to remember that even if we think we're living safe and healthy lives, any of these horrific and unexpected third-party tragedies (outside of our control) can befall upon us at any time. It is always important to appreciate the time you have because you just never know when it will come to an unnatural end. We certainly all hope for a natural end well into our golden years, but we have to start thinking and becoming aware at a very young age that time is precious and not guaranteed.

It is important to start to think in this manner because it automatically forces you to take active control and power of your life. When you have a genuine understanding of time and its precarious nature, you start to hustle, you get your butt in gear, right? For example, how often at work have you hustled in the last hour of your day before your day ends? You weren't productive most of the day, but in that last hour you suddenly realize you have to get some work done. When you feel and are aware of the minutes ticking away, you actually start living in the moment without realizing. We have to treat every hour of our twenty-four-hour day like it's our last hour on earth. We have to "feel" those seconds and minutes coarse through our bodies. Think about the mere fact that the few seconds it took you just to read this paragraph alone, you will never get those seconds back in your life. Isn't that crazy to conceptualize? You'll never recover those elapsed seconds. I certainly hope I didn't waste your seconds.

How do we get to the point where we consistently appreciate time on a daily basis, not take it for granted, and ultimately feel like you've accomplished something by the end of the day? You have to routinely acknowledge the many little examples throughout the day that remind you that time is precious and that time has passed by. The most obvious and precise example we have is time itself. In other words, what time is it right now? Physically looking at and noticing what time it is, whether on your phone, watch, clock, etc. is the most common form of time awareness. Every time you look at and notice the actual time of day, you have to acknowledge that a certain number of minutes or hours have passed since the last time you checked. Did you feel that it was time well spent during that elapsed period? When you have breaks during the day, such as breakfast, lunch and dinner, you're enjoying that break with the people you're with, but you are not consciously aware of the time itself passing. When you're watching a show or a movie, are you aware of the minutes and hours elapsing? Are you spending them in a way where you feel you had quality time? Or do you feel like you wasted time? Do you feel the elapsing and wasting of time when you're stuck in traffic and the minutes are ticking off, when you're in an elevator and the seconds are counting down, or when you're endlessly scrolling through social media? There are so many daily reminders and examples of time elapsing.

We are in control of the choice of how to spend those minutes and hours, but often times, we're not consciously aware of all the time that has expired.

You just have to start becoming more actively aware of time. For example, I'm cautious of the second hand moving on my wrist-watch and I keep my eye on it. I've also set my cell phone to show the seconds next to the minutes and hours. This way I'm always within visual sight of seconds counting down. The more you become aware of time, the more it is ingrained into your involuntary way of think-ing. Once that happens, you're hooked. You become a time lover, a time apologist, and a time fan, if you will. You start realizing that time is better spent in other ways. You start foregoing some of the things you used to do in order to spend more quality time on other things. Your friends, family, spouse, and children are placed higher on your list of priorities and quality time spent. You start getting up earlier in the mornings, hitting the gym more often, and taking advantage of the limited hours you know you have in one day. You try to extend your day by being more active. Sometimes I start my day so early in the morning and include so much in it, that by the end of this day, it feels like I've experienced two days' worth.

You include more people in your life with the time spent. You start visiting your friends and family more. You start taking better care of yourself to improve your longevity and thus have more time in the future. You start to appreciate and enjoy life more. You stop being a workaholic because you know that not only is it taking away time spent with others, but it is slowly making you unhealthy. In short, your quality and enjoyment of life improves and expands. Your choices of time spent improve significantly.

In addition to the daily reminders and examples of time we all have in our lives, there is a larger example of time that we've created as a form of entertainment — sports. Sports are a great microcosm of life and time in many respects. Every single type of sport has time as its final and ultimate endpoint. When the final seconds of time count down to zero, an exalted victor is declared. We are all witness to this countdown, the last out, or the last set of a match. The incredible exhilaration that fans feel when the end is near is greatly palpable. It evokes and imitates a life and death scenario. The final buzzer beater that declares a champion is a lightning bolt of ecstasy. In the end, there is a winner and loser; there is the ultimate high of winning and the agony of losing. But because sports never have a literal end/death, the next day, or the next season, the game continues, and so do we, in our quest for excitement. The game of life, however, is not like that. The end can be sudden and tragic, and unfortunately, there are no winners. Sadly, most of us don't realize that fragility. It's time that we did.

"Time is the most valuable thing a man can spend."

THEOPHRASTUS

STAGE 3:

Change is the
Constant Currency

With every passing second of time, a change occurs. Life has permanently changed in that very next second. There is no way to go back to *un-change* it. Changes occur a million times more than we realize. Yet when we do take notice, it's usually because we are opposed to change. Why is that? Why are we opposed to something that is constantly happening around us? You've certainly changed, as I have. I'm sure you weren't the same person yesterday, or even a few hours ago. But no one is confronting you about it are they? They're not asking you to go back to the person you were yesterday.

While time is our priceless commodity, change is the one constant we have in our lives. Change is the currency that never fluctuates. It always remains the same and it is always there. Like water and time, it remains fluid and ever-flowing, not to be altered or impeded in any way by human attempts, or any attempts for that matter. But most importantly, change is ultimately good, and it is needed in the long run of life, even it doesn't feel like it in the moment sometimes.

It's amazing that so many people do not acknowledge its state of being or its state of constant movement. These are people who live in the past and are afraid to face their truths. They ignore, deny, and defy change, yet they are quick to blame change for their perceived negative experiences. They don't even realize or give credit to the fact that if change didn't exist, life wouldn't exist, that our physical bodies wouldn't exist. Our cells are constantly changing, growing, and replicating in order for life to sustain and continue. Ironically, our vigilant defiance of change is completely antithetical and oxymoron-ish because while we're fighting to survive in spite of change, we don't realize that our survival is based on it. We are constantly paddling upstream, swimming against the current, sailing against the wind, and pushing the giant boulder up the mountain. Instead of simply letting go and floating with the wind of change, we're determined to destroy its unstoppable lava flow, and inevitably become buried and burned by it.

The primary reason why most people are so averse to change has to do with mankind's original survival-based default psyche. Ancient humans had to literally survive on a daily basis and constantly face their fears of death. Our original fear-based and survival-based instincts and thoughts are still ingrained in the minds of modern-day humans. Even though daily survival is no longer a facet of modern human civilizations, the fear-based psychology is still there. Consequently, whenever we see something or someone different than what we're accustomed, our initial default response is one of fear and survival instead of curiosity and love. That is why change appears in the form of fear to us instead of an opportunity and explanation of new life. That is also why man's entrenched hatred (i.e. racism) exists. We fear what looks and sounds different to us instead of opening our arms and asking questions about our differences. We'll also cover this topic at a later Stage.

However, once we become aware of the fact that we can override our default, instinctual reactions and thoughts, we're able to pause and create new thoughts and ways of viewing the unknown. We become understanding and accepting of the reasons behind change and we begin to share this awareness with others so they can also take advantage of the opportunities that come with change. We have the intelligence, awareness, and wisdom to circumvent our entrenched thoughts in order to arrive at the correct understanding of any given situation. We are obligated to do so. It would be foolish, selfish, and arrogant of us not to think beyond what we've come to know leading up to the encounter of something new and different from the prior norm.

That's how new norms are formed. That's how evolution happens. Can you imagine if all life forms, animals, and humans fought change and evolution since the beginning of time? We would last maybe one day, if that. Beautiful butterflies wouldn't exist, they would die as caterpillars. The simple, round-about lesson is that change should be embraced with open arms, an open heart, and inquisitive mind, not with a closed mind and clenched arms. To that end, I have developed a relatable formula for change that we can follow in our everyday lives as follows.

A FORMULA FOR BEING ONE WITH CHANGE

Change = Constant/Inevitable/Opportunities/New Life

Fear = Resistance/Frustration/Anger/Resentment/Hatred

Fear Opposes Change

Deleting Fear = Being Open/Approaching with Love/Childhood Innocence/Curious

Downloading Love = Embracing Opportunities from Change

Opportunities = Change in Yourself/Change in Others/Living More of Life

We are born with Love, not Fear.

Fear replaces Love as we grow into adulthood (if we let it).

Change is immortal and immutable, we are not.

Deleting Fear and re-installing innocent Love makes us one with Change, thus making our Legacy immortal and immutable.

Stop resisting change. Get accustomed and conditioned in your mind's eye to view every instance of change as an opportunity, an awareness, a revelation of some type that will directly benefit your life if you let it. Swim in the same direction of the flow of this change. One of my peeves is when many people inevitably use the trite expression, "Remember the good old days?" What good old days exactly? There's no such thing. People have had to fabricate a misconception that things and life were better in the past. Really? How far back are we going to the good old days? You want to go back to the days of no cars, no technology, no running water or plumbing, no freedoms for oppressed people (we're still working on that one), etc.? What they really mean is that they want to go back in a way where they can pick and choose the things they like about the past and leave behind the things they don't. They want to create their own buffet of life and only place on their plates their favorites for consumption. Wouldn't that be just peachy? Life doesn't work that way. You don't get to pick and choose aspects of life from the past in defiance of today's wave of change.

They use this false trope to create commiseration with you because they don't understand what is happening and why it is happening. They literally take it personally, choosing to believe that change can only be bad for them because of their own warped perspective. They don't understand because they've allowed their fear to block their open mind from understanding and seeing the natural perspective of change, the progressive flow of change. They are completely stuck in the past when thinking this way. That's why they long and wish for the "good old days" of this false past.

Some people are so stuck in the past that their immediate reaction to change is one of a false sense of righteous indignation. They speak angrily of this feared change as if it's an abomination on them. This is an undeveloped and an entitled way of thinking and behaving. Mature adults should not carry a false sense of righteous indignation. There's nothing to be initially angry about for no reason simply because you feel that you have an automatic stake in the matter. Falsely believing that you have an undeniable say on the matter simply because you have lived long enough to know a different life from the past is not justifiable. The reason is because your defiance of the change comes from a fear of the unknown (caused by your indignation) instead of rational thought.

However, there is a type of change that may not initially seem like it is in the best interest for all in the greater sense. Sometimes what can happen in life is a change that is extreme and reactionary in nature. It is one that desires to correct a heinous wrong or a great injustice. But this reactionary change occurs so quickly that it tends to over-correct the wrong in a way that it justifiably angers those that were innocently and negatively affected by this extreme change of over-correction. It is a change that was effected without the complete consideration and analysis of all ramifications. When this happens, patience must be at the forefront, as hard as it may be in the moment to have such patience. Life has a way of correcting over-corrections and coming back to the mean of even balance. Consequently, the very next change that follows the extreme one corrects the over-compensation. Patience is key in this situation. However, you can also be a conduit for the next needed change of even balance, so long as you are genuine in your efforts in keeping with the spirit of the original change. In other words, you're not trying to obliterate all forms of this change with your selfish agenda of reverting back to exactly how things were.

It probably never occurred to you, but all of the great innovators, inventors, creators, philosophers, leaders, etc. from both our ancient and modern civilizations, have one common trait that links them all together. And that is, they embraced change. In fact, they saw change coming and took that opportunity to create all of the inventions of mankind that we take for granted today. From the time the wheel was invented to the modern-day iPhone, they were all created because their creators had the vision of change at the top of their minds. They all chose to be as one within the flow of change itself. They had the awareness that the best approach to change was to catch it and ride it, just like the perfect wave. Can you imagine a world where our most intelligent innovators had been operating from fear and were completely closed-minded to change? We would still be foolishly trying to roll a square wheel. Suffer the Neanderthal fool who would suggest such a thing, even more so the fool who follows.

"It is not the strongest of the species that survive, nor the most intelligent, but the one most responsive to change."

CHARLES DARWIN

STAGE 4:

The Power of Your Mind

Have you ever considered how much power your mind holds? This is my most favorite and exciting Stage, the one where your potential and reality meet. This is the Stage that will blow your mind and help you gain an unlimited level of confidence and certainty when you grasp the sheer power and control you have with your mind.

While humans are part of the animal kingdom, we are miles apart from other animals simply because we possess an analytical, limitless mind. Absolutely everything we know as humans starts and ends with our minds, our brain to be more specific. The power of your mind will ALWAYS allow you (or at least give you the opportunity) to willfully and purposefully control every aspect of your life in the exact manner you desire, or at least in the exact manner within your immediate control.

Life is ultimately about choices, right? You have to be in control of those choices 24/7. You have to hold the power of your choices and never relinquish them. The only person in this world that you can rely on 100% without equivocation is yourself, which in truth, is really your mind. Many people like to blame others or circumstances for the aspects of their lives that don't go their way. We all know that no one other than yourself can and should be blamed for your choices. No matter how influenced by external forces and pressure, ultimately you are the one who's made them and has to live with them. Why do we routinely pass the blame and accountability to someone or something else? Well, it's because we're in denial and we're not able to face the truths in our lives. Doing so exposes us to the lives we're not living. But the first step to taking ownership of our minds, and therefore our lives, is acknowledging the incredible power that we hold. Every single person has an amazing, unlimited mind whose potential is untapped.

Tremendous strength and confidence comes from harnessing the immeasurable will power that we have. Whoever created the human body made an absolutely divine, complex, and resourceful, yet an incredibly easy-to-use brain. Our brain is an endless buffet of resources that is user-friendly and can be accessed at a second's notice. We hold the power of perspective. We can view any situation, decision, dilemma, challenge, etc. in any perspective that we desire. The key is to find that right perspective that opens the door to many opportunities and solutions. You can either choose to view a situation from an inherent negative perspective, which most of us are prone to, or you can pause and realize that there's a 180-degree perspective that when taken, opens your eyes to the truth of the situation. Having the mental fortitude and awareness in the precise moment to be able to pause and re-align your pre-programmed thinking into a new way of thinking is what needs to happen. It's difficult to do, but can be mastered and installed as your default mechanism when practiced repeatedly, daily, and over time.

The most beautiful and re-assuring part is that our brain is always ON, 24/7, without fail. It never sleeps or turns off, even when we are sleeping. It is man's ultimate best and most loyal friend. It is literally always there for you. Even if you try to turn it off, you can't. It won't let you. I've certainly tried. How can you not use it to your advantage? How can you not use it in ways to maximize your potential, all the time, every day? Well, sadly, many of us don't. We take our mind for granted, like many other parts of our lives. I'm here to wake up your mind and remind you that you can and should be using the most precious resource you have much more often than you've ever thought possible.

When you do so, meaning take complete ownership of your mind and harness its power potential, you will always feel a heightened state of all your senses. You will know what being truly awake feels like because you will literally feel the wave of energy coursing through your body. You will feel intense excitement every time you visualize the moment of your future reality being realized. You will always be hopeful and positive about that future reality. The most important facet of this aspect is to always approach every single situation of your life with your kid's-like exuberance, energy, innocence, and imagination. You have to feel like you're having fun as a kid because adults forget how to have fun. Express your kid's enjoyment, don't suppress it. When you approach life, particularly the challenging moments, with a kid's-like innocence of exuberance and enthusiasm, the stigma of the challenge disappears and the process becomes easier to manage. You approach every challenge with a smile instead of a stern face of concern. You're not worried about the outcome because you're lost in the fun of the moment's actions.

Tom Brady, for example, has frequently commented that when he plays the game, he reminds himself to do so as a kid, and to always remember to have fun. When you're in a child's mind, you don't know much more than what's happening in the moment. It is a great way to tap into the innocence of the moment without judgment or expectations. That thought process has been instrumental to Tom Brady's consistent success.

The first step of taking complete ownership of your mind is not easy to do. You have been programmed from birth by every external influence that exists, from your parents, friends, media, religious leaders, society, governments, etc. At birth, you need their influence because you cannot survive as a child on your own. But as you grow into young adulthood and your mind starts to take shape, you take on the almost impossible task of genuinely thinking for yourself. This requires you to be honest with the learned truths you've known versus the truths that you begin to shape for yourself. It is very difficult to start diverging from your path and potentially defy the people that raised you if they do not agree with your new line of thinking. That is why most people continue to live their lives according to what they have been taught, without analyzing if it is true or correct.

For example, if you grew up in an environment where hate was fostered, you will probably live your life as someone who hates others as well. It is very difficult to break a cycle or pattern that's been so ingrained by your upbringing and environment. But if you want to live your authentic life, you have to be able to break that cycle and pattern. That requires you to use your diagnostic mind and come to life-changing and ground-breaking decisions about what you believe and who you are. Only you can do that. The decisions you make from the power of your mind are permanently yours without recourse to any external pressure of any kind or influence from another, which means they are more permanent and without regret. The power resides in you and in your mind.

Once you're able to master this first most challenging step of taking 100% ownership of the power of your mind, all the other steps easily fall in line and present themselves to you in plain sight. But you have to be fully convinced and believe that your mind is completely yours and that no one else or thing will have any power or influence over it. You have to cherish and guard your power of your mind as much as you would your own actual life. When someone physically threatens your life for example, you instinctively try to defend your life as a survival reaction. You wouldn't think twice about that. In the same way, when someone tries to influence or control your mind, you have to doggedly defend that takeover just as much because the survival of your true self depends on it. Giving up control of your mind to another is the equivalent of victimizing yourself in such a manner that you believe there's no escaping your environment.

It's not easy spotting a takeover of your mind as it usually occurs slowly over a period of grooming and/or brainwashing. You are systematically told lies over and over such that they become normalized. The lies lose their shock value, causing you to become anaesthetized to them. When enough people lie and make false promises, then words stop meaning anything. There are no more answers and truths, just better and better lies. They form new truths for you and don't appear false to you anymore. This process doesn't necessarily have to be in a formal setting such as an institution, an affiliation or the most blatant example, such a cult. It could merely be the environment that you're raised in or decide to partake at a point in your life when your young mind is till forming. However, the unfortunate and greatest risk when allowing your mind to be groomed or brainwashed is that it becomes akin to an addiction from which you are physically no longer able to extract yourself. Third-party intervention is needed, and even then, it's an extremely difficult process to re-gain control of your brainwashed mind. Once you're in a world which you thought was made of your own creation, you see no logical reason to defy it because your unbreakable attachment feels like a natural and innate one of your doing.

Repeated lies that become truths in your mind are the most insidious forms of false truths that form a dogma in your trapped mind. Most of George Orwell's writings for example, were based on this theme as he fervently tried to convey and expose to the world how normal this had become in society. The good news is that this is all completely avoidable when your mind is instinctively prepared to defend itself because of the power you hold. You're able to see real and genuine human truths clearly, and can immediately spot false truths miles before they approach your domain.

Once you have fully placed yourself in a permanent mental state of complete power and control of your mind, the next level of harnessing your mind power is to be vigilantly observant of life happening in front of your eyes, on a daily basis. In other words, remain and be silent as often as possible and take in every observation of daily existence around you. An important Buddhist proverb states, "Don't speak if it doesn't improve on silence." When you're silent and observing, that's when you're learning, that's when education happens and epiphanies are materialized. That's also when you start seeing truths from falsehoods. When other people are doing all the talking, let them talk away. That is when you are able to peak behind their curtain to see who they really are and what they believe. You're not only learning from what they are saying, but you're learning from what they are not saying, their choice of phrasing, their word choices, and their body language. The more you remain silent as a fervent observer, the more they will talk and the more you learn in the process. People rush to fill silences because it makes them feel uncomfortable. When they're uncomfortable, inadvertent truths reveal themselves.

When you become accustomed to this daily observational behavior, human trends and tendencies become readily apparent to you. You will become hyper-observant and keenly perceptive. Every little detail becomes more prominent. Once this happens, you are able to make real-time analyses and determinations of the truths and falsehoods you are observing. You will form your own credible truths based on these analyses, which will start the process of breaking down some of the learned truths from your upbringing and prior education systems. The learned and behavioral truths of your past are not necessarily false, nor do you need to unlearn them. However, you are now in position to intellectually ask yourself valid and necessary questions in order to reconcile your learned truths from the past with your new truths of today. These constant and periodic reconciliations in your life and of your life become a normal part of your intellectual thought process.

Once you've mastered the ability to (1) take control and strengthen the power of your mind and (2) re-align your way of thinking through silence and keen and insightful observation, the most important aspect of unlocking and harnessing the pure power you possess is to defy one aspect of your mind over the other to awaken critical thought. Here's what I mean. I'm not talking about your rational mind versus your creative mind. They are both tremendously equally important, and we will cover this aspect at a later Stage. What I'm talking about is the most often defaulted aspect of our minds with which people think — and that is what I call our easy mind (or lazy if you will). This is our reactively driven mind. In most aspects of our lives, it is human nature to take the easy way out, a shortcut, to find a way that makes any process or decision easier. Because of this human tendency, we most often resort to thinking with our easy/lazy mind at almost every decision point in our lives. While this can be helpful and useful, especially when an absolute and immediate life-saving or life-altering decision needs to be made in the critical moment, it is usually the wrong thought process for critical thinking.

Most people think reactively because it requires no effort. It's the easy route. The goal is to start thinking proactively as often as possible. Instead of instantly responding to someone or something without any forethought, you must pause and absorb both the totality of the situation and the all-encompassing specific details of it, without judgment and pre-disposed assumptions. You have to assess every detail at its face value, without judgment, while diagnosing the reasons, causes, and ramifications of every detail during your in-the-moment experience. Most assumptions are usually wrong because you don't have all the information to know what you think you know. Therefore you cannot have any assumptions, which can result in bias. Bias results in incorrect and false assessments. People have a natural tendency to fill empty spaces and silences, and therefore create incorrect assumptions. After this pause of awareness, you are able to formulate proactive thoughts and responses. This process will become easier over time, and it will consequently become instinctual and habitual.

The easy/reactive mind needs to be re-programmed over time to become your habitual, proactive method of thinking, what I call your diagnostic mind. The diagnostic mind is the one that analyzes any given situation or decision point systematically, logically and truthfully. In other words, your mind is constantly and routinely diagnosing every situation and decision to arrive at a clear answer(s) and/or clear options and paths. The diagnostic mind inherently looks for reasons and root causes within the details as it diagnoses for answers. It is so easy and routine to immediately respond to someone or to a situation without thinking diagnostically. In other words, we're usually lazy of mind and want to come to a quick decision. However, in that moment, this is precisely when we should be pausing to assess and diagnose the situation in order to arrive at the proper response or decision. When we do so, we avoid many potential negative situations, the ramifications of which could be devastating.

The more often you pause without acting and responding, the more you start to strengthen this diagnostic muscle of your brain. Beyond just the knowledge that you've gained in life thru education systems, thinking analytically for yourself with a greater sense of awareness will help you naturally develop a higher level of emotional intelligence. Emotional intelligence cannot be taught. You have to develop and strengthen this important mind muscle on your own using empathy as your central core. Developing and changing your though process to channel and merge with your emotional intelligence on a consistent basis will become the template of your diagnostic mind, which will ultimately help you gain wisdom. Knowledge plus emotional intelligence plus critical thinking results in wisdom.

Just like we can train our physical body and muscles to effect growth and gains, we can do the same with our minds. In fact, the more you train your mind, the more your world opens up. It's amazing how vastly you start thinking on much broader, wider, and deeper levels. You start thinking not just one step ahead or two steps, you start thinking ten, twenty steps ahead. You can see ramifications and responses so easily. You can out-think or out-wit anyone or anything because you're always thinking at a level that is many steps ahead of your counter point. You understand the given moment in such a heightened and intense way, that your mind is burning and exploding with thoughts that you want to convey and share with the world. Details become so vivid and clear, the systematic approach to problem-solving becomes so evident, and the road you're traveling becomes the Autobahn of answers, with no traffic in sight to thwart you from your destination point. You look forward to challenges, you start multi-tasking regularly to challenge you, you become hyper-focused, and you want to be as productive as possible on a daily basis. Your mind is always out-thinking the other person or any given situation, not because you have to but because it's become a normal way to process everything. Harnessing the power of your mind in this way is the ultimate natural high of life, a high that you will feel often and regularly.

No one can ever take that power away from you. It is your super power. It is the best super power a human can have, in fact, the only super power we have, since none of us can be the actual Superman or Batman, etc. Frankly, after I learned how to harness my own super mind power, I would never want to be anything or anyone but my true self. My confidence is undeterred and my determination is like a bullet train steadfastly blazing on permanent tracks. When you feel this way, you naturally exude your passion, vibrancy, and mission, along with a big smile on your face to the people around you, without even realizing. And that is because you're simply being your true self at this point and nothing more. Other people will take notice and they will be magnetically drawn to you because they will see you as the leader-type with genuine and noble qualities. This is when you'll know that you've truly mastered your mind's power and when you'll feel obligated to share your wisdom with others. The best part is that it won't feel like an obligation to share, the sharing will automatically start pouring out of you because you'll have an authentic concern and care for people.

Lastly, the greatest benefit in your life (in addition to the benefit of helping people) will be that you can now use your will power to effect literally any change in your life. For example, because your mind's power is so strong now, you can extract yourself from any addiction, including the ones that require third-party medical intervention. The extraction process starts with your undeniable and impenetrable commitment to want to change, therefore, the rest of the process becomes obligatory and rudimentary. You will be committed to seeing it through no matter the level of difficulty and pain. You will be a great student to any 12-step type process without going off-course. Making other less challenging changes will not be a problem, and you'll make them at a drop of a hat because you've simply told your mind to do so. And the reason why this will be easy is because your mind will know and stay loyal to the cold and immutable truths. In other words, you won't be able to deviate and/ or be in denial of the truths you know because of your strong will power. You cannot defy yourself any longer because this defiance will clash like a Category 5 hurricane with your real and genuine new self. Dropping bad habits will become normal and compulsory like an animal shedding its unneeded skin.

On a daily basis, as you're going about your day from the time you wake up, your mind will be in a constant state of preparation, meaning that you will involuntarily start thinking about all the little details of the given day and the near future in a way that your mind will plan and prepare you for the day. It will be almost impossible to turn it off, but your mind will be constantly mapping out, bullet-pointing for you, reminding you, visualizing for you, and preparing you for every task and every facet of detail. You'll feel as confident as a prepared, veteran quarterback, easily splicing through a defense that is many steps behind. This constant, mind-on-a-reel, thought process will even get annoying sometimes because it will prepare and visualize you for the most mundane things of your every-day routine, like taking a shower, what you're going to eat, the workout at the gym, etc. But it will also prepare you almost word for word, and action for action, for the day's events. Your mind will always be ahead of you in this way so you'll never have to actively try to think or ponder on a matter, or remind yourself of anything. It will start the process for you.

For example, if you have a presentation to give at work, a discussion you know you'll be having with a co-worker, or a meeting in which you will be a participant, your mind will be outlining the narrative for you almost word for word. You'll always be confident and ready in these situations because your mind has prepared you with a game plan. Your situational awareness will be greatly heightened. You will always be operating from a base of your combined effect of being acutely observational and having a heightened situational awareness. After any given situation or experience, your mind will always analyze and assess how you did. It will play back for you the important details so that you'll be able to learn from your mistakes and take pride in your successes. Just don't be too hard on yourself when your mind starts over-analyzing your mistakes. It can turn to doubt and being too critical. Keep the focus to learning from them, not repeating them, then simply moving on.

There's a consistent efficiency that comes with thinking proactively and diagnostically. Because you become a proficient and efficient thinker on the fly, the ways in which you live your life and go about your daily process also become efficient. You don't waste time anymore, you are methodical, you plan, and you are able to easily see the spaces and gaps of your daily living that need to be reconciled and accounted. In other words, you start living your life by shortening the distance from point A to point B. You're able to see the tangible, visible straight line from A to B. There is no curved, meandering line anymore. Most people live their lives without this sense of tangible, focused direction, and therefore without efficiency and proficiency. In no way however, is this efficiency a linear way of thinking, far from it. It is simply another benefit of how clear and effective one becomes with the diagnostic mind.

This type of consistent and clear-headed thinking also significantly reduces and almost completely eliminates (over time) negative thoughts and doubting self-talk. It is scientifically proven that when our mind is idle and has free reign, it is more likely to focus on negative thought patterns than positive ones. Because of our ancestral survival-based instincts, our mind is programmed to prioritize safety and anticipate danger, which can result in negative thought patterns and self-doubt. When you allow your mind to be as idle as a painted ship on a painted ocean, it can become difficult to focus on the positive aspects of your life because you've allowed your mind to focus on pre-programmed survival rather than intentional forethought. However, once you harness the power of your mind and take firm control of it, there is virtually no more allowance for mind idleness. Idleness will be replaced by intentional contemplation and fore-thought.

You will talk to your mind routinely and tell it many things. I do this regularly. It is the way I utilize my will power and my mind's power. You will have a real relationship with your mind, one of clear and precise communication. For example, I told my mind about twenty-five years ago that I would completely stop using an alarm clock in the mornings to wake up, that there was no need for it anymore. I dropped my alarm clock cold turkey from that day forward by simply telling my mind each prior evening what time I wanted to wake the next morning. I've since been waking up on my own at almost precisely the time I had set in my mind. I've done this without fail, and have literally never overslept. Many times, I even wake up precisely to the minute of my desired time, truly uncanny. Other times I wake up a half hour or so before the designated time, but rarely past the desired time. I'm able to snooze effectively as well if I decide to do so. I'll simply tell my mind to wake again in five minutes and I do.

Another example of talking to my mind to effect a change is when I stopped drinking all forms of soda, cold turkey, about twenty years ago. That was one less unhealthy habit instantly eliminated. I had no trouble telling my mind to effect this change on a permanent basis, and I haven't had one soda since. Ultimately, it is simply a matter of a committed choice that you are making. The difference now is that your mind is easily prepared and ready to effect any change for you.

I've also utilized the healing powers of my mind, which I do believe exist. I have told my mind on many occasions to recover faster from the flu for example. At times, when I catch it in time, I've told my mind not to get sick when I feel something coming on, and it has usually worked. I believe that the mind is able to send healing signals to the rest of your body to affect a faster recovery and/or eliminate the ailment. While this takes repetitive practice combined with being highly in tune with your physical body, it can be achieved in time. What I mean about being in tune with your body is that when all three phases of your health are synchronized and working efficiently with each other, you become mentally and physically as one with your body and mind. You are acutely aware of your health and actual physical condition and are able to self-diagnose yourself most times.

When these three phases of your health of consistent physical activity, proper nutrition, and adequate sleep are in sync, you develop a keen awareness and understanding of how your body operates and reacts to everyday living. Once this is achieved, you can start talking to your mind to send healing signals when you feel ill or have a particular ailment. I usually do this for several minutes in bed right before going to sleep. Most times it works, depending on how strongly I am concentrating and committed to this task. I realize the placebo effect may be in play, but that's precisely the point isn't it? Whether or not your brain is chemically sending healing signals is no longer the point. The result and effect of healing is the point. It is a way to self-manifest healing. Self-manifestation becomes more possible when you harness the power of your mind in these ways.

Another way to understand the ability to condition our mind to a new way of thinking is the knowledge that our mind will always protect us no matter what. Because we still possess innate survival instincts, your mind will always condition itself to protect you mentally, so that you can manage your life physically without going insane, essentially. Take for example, the concept of Stockholm Syndrome, derived from the concentration camps of the Jewish Holocaust. This is a situation when a person is forced, through no free will of their own, to be enslaved and imprisoned in an incarcerated environment. The mind realizes that you have to be able to cope and survive such an extreme, traumatic, and harsh scenario. It starts to normalize these abhorrent actions and situations so that you can become accustomed to it and manage your stress and coping mechanism. In other words, you have to survive this situation for as long as necessary. This is your mind's way of protecting you from the mental debilitation and breakdown from the trauma being inflicted upon you.

If your mind is able to protect you in such a significant and magnificent way based on its own *involuntary* conditioning mechanism, think of what you are capable of when you are directly and *voluntarily* conditioning your mind. When you consider that you are voluntarily re-programming your default thinking process from a reactive to a diagnostic way of thinking, you are forcing this new conditioning onto yourself in a way that your life depends on it, because it does. If you truly believe that your life will be a better one as a result, you should approach this conditioning process as a solution and answer to a simulated life-and-death situation, one in which you tell yourself you have no choice but to do it. Not giving yourself an out, in this manner, keeps you disciplined and on course.

There are many examples in my life of actively utilizing my will power. Fortunately for me, I stayed away from addictive enticements and behaviors starting at a very young age. I don't have a story to tell you of overcoming an addiction, for example. I've honestly lived an entirely healthy lifestyle since a young age without deviating. I've stayed true to the healthy principles of proper nutrition, going to the gym every day, and getting quality sleep every night. As I've mentioned before, once I learned these truths to be self-evident at a young age, why would I ever deviate from them? They comprise my constitution. Once you realize these truths to be self-evident in your own process, no matter what stage or age of your life, you will not deviate either. That is the ultimate beauty of the power of your mind. Once you have full and relentless grasp of it, it will never let you down in any way. It will be your best and most unconditional friend forever, without fail, if you let it.

"A great man is hard on himself. A small man is hard on others."

CONFUCIUS

"Failure is success in progress."

ALBERT EINSTEIN

STAGE 5:

Transcend Your Personal History

Who are you? The real question is who were you? Who was the person that was formed in your likeness that we see today based on the history you experienced? That is the point of origin where you must start.

Transcending your personal history is the most important Stage for growth and development as a self-actualized individual. Most people don't ever break the negative cycle of their upbringing primarily because they wrongly believe they are not capable of effecting any significant change in their life. However, it is crucially important for people to understand and firmly believe that regardless of your heritage, history, child rearing, and environment, breaking your chains and transcending your own personal history is not only possible, but it is necessary in the quest to find your true identity.

As children, we unfortunately do not possess the critical thinking skills or the control of our lives to even have any sense that perhaps we're not being raised in the proper environment. Sadly for many people, the experiences, modelling, and behaviors we live through as children are believed to be normal and accepted. They form and shape our early identities, lives, and life patterns. However, once we grow to an age to where our critical thinking abilities become an important asset in the future direction of our lives, we are in position to finally take control of our identity and life. The age when this becomes a new reality of thinking obviously differs for each person. But the frailty of this realization does not make for an easy decision for a young adult to decide to defy their history and start forging a new path.

This realization is not an easy one to accept. It forces you to not only realize that your life to this point has not been the best one, but to make a decision about what you're going to do now with this new found awareness. Thus the frailty of the realization puts you in a delicate balance of deciding which one of the two paths you will travel—the path paved with your familiar and familial history or the newly created one begging you to take steps towards it. For most people, the shocking awareness and realization at such a young adult age is almost impossible to handle. This is why it is so difficult for us to break the patterns, to break the chains, and forge a new life that we know is within us. This is why many people do not do it. For many, it is extremely difficult to grasp and accept the notion that your history needs to be destroyed, or at least significantly altered, for you to become the person you know you should be. This overwhelming thought places you in immediate self-denial mode. Thus you continue with your same life, living the same patterns and ultimately passing along these negative patterns to your children. You allow the cycle to continue, unbroken in your life, and unfortunately, in the future lives of your children. Will they be strong enough to break the cycle?

However, for those of us who are strong enough to face these burning truths of our fragile existence begin to steer a different course for our lives. It doesn't have to be in the form of (and typically isn't) a grand formal announcement with pomp and circumstance declaring your victorious annihilation of your chains. It usually begins quietly and slowly while you continue to grasp and understand the momentous personal decision you've just made that will shape the rest of your life. It will be both scary and overwhelming, yet it will be underpinned with the calming knowledge and awareness that you're doing the right thing, which will serve as your inner strength to continue and forge forward. You may or may not have to forsake members of your family and/or inner circle of friends. This depends, of course, on the severity of the issues in your upbringing and inner members of your environment. For many of us, you can still have and maintain loving and respectful relationships with your family and friends with the clear knowledge that you have made and chosen a different life for yourself than the one from which you came. For some, forsaking your entire prior life of family and/or friends will be sadly necessary for you to completely leave your demons in the past.

Using my upbringing as an example, I grew up in an environment of extreme alcoholism and pernicious domestic violence. My father was a terrible example of a parent and person. He was a raging and violent alcoholic who made my mother's and our lives horrible. However, at a very young toddler age, I was fortunate enough to have some sort of awareness that this was not the way our lives should be. I was able to discern and decide at a young age that my father was 100% wrong in the way he lived his life and the one he created for our victimized family. I clearly remember making a firm decision as a child of about five years of age that if I simply grow up to be the complete opposite of this person representing to be my father, that I would have a chance to be a decent person. I also remember making the decision to not be a drinker, and certainly not to be a physically and emotionally abusive person. As I grew older, this decision was made more concrete in my mind.

Additionally, I decided to break all of what I believed to be unhealthy and unloving negative patterns of my environment. I felt proud of my decisions and made it known to my family. I grew up having hatred for my father and didn't want anything to do with him. I was ashamed of even mentioning that I had a father like him. I made sure that I would live a life of being a loving, caring, and empathetic person to every single person in my life, starting with my family and friends, and always placing their needs and lives above mine. When my father died, I finally made the decision to let go of the anger and hatred I had for him. I realized that I had to do that for my own sanity and peace of mind. I genuinely forgave him while realizing and accepting that he was a product of his own generation, and that he simply did not have the strength and courage to break his own chains. He didn't know that he didn't have to live with his demons. He didn't know that demons are just inflated balloon bullies who need to be punched in the face to be deflated and eradicated.

While transcending your history is important in the process of exposing and solidifying your true identity, I know that this does not apply to people who were raised in caring, nurturing environments, and were supported in their entire lives in the most encouraging and loving ways. My wife was fortunate to grow up in such a household. I know that there are loving families who raise their children in the healthiest environments possible. My family that I've created with my marriage and children is like that. My children have grown to be amazing and loving adults, each of whom has forged a path of true and genuine identity for herself, with the consistent and full support and encouragement of their parents. As I mentioned, my wife was also raised in a loving family of several siblings and the same set of parents married for over sixty-five years. When I met my wife and saw the family in which she was raised, I knew that was exactly what I wanted, which was the complete antithesis of my upbringing. Because my wife was raised in an ideal family and I had a concept in my mind of such a family (by breaking the cycle of mine), creating a healthy one for our children was easy and straightforward. She was raised with the proper parental modeling her entire life and I knew what that should look like. Thus, it was self-evident to know how to properly parent and raise our children.

It is important to reiterate, that no matter at what point you are in your life currently, it is imperative that you transcend your history to forge your own true path, one that will bring you fulfillment and peace as a result of your transcendence. Even if you didn't have the strength to do so as a young adult, you have the maturity, wisdom, and strength to do it now. It is never too late. As long you're still alive, you have the ability and will power to face the harsh truths of who you are and how you were formed by your history. You can start chipping away and destroying the facets of that history that you know do not represent who you are. From a logical standpoint, why would you want to hold on to the negative aspects of what formed you? It doesn't make sense. I realize it's easier to make such a statement than effectuating the needed changes. But it starts in small steps. The first step is total and complete awareness and acknowledgement of the demons that you need to punch in the face. Once you have that, the decisions become easier to make and the demons start fluttering away in the wind without too much effort thereafter.

Even if you know that you haven't completely transcended your history because you haven't yet started or you're currently in the process of it, your life is definitely going in the right direction if you're experiencing some or all of the following. If you have the following in your life, you're on the right track of effecting permanent changes by breaking your chains.

a.   You have supportive people in your life. You feel good about not just your family members, but the inner circle of your trusted friends and confidants. And you also know the people from whom you need to steer away.

b. You know the changes that need to be made in your life. You've come to certain realizations in your life and you've placed yourself on a path of making those changes.

c. You have a better sense of balance in your life and you habitually seek this balance. You're not living life in the extremes. You realize that extreme behaviors and habits can be unhealthy and unfulfilling.

d. While you haven't figured everything out yet, you're happy with who you are at this point in your life. You're content about how you feel about yourself, but you're striving for more awareness. You feel like you're learning and growing every day. Even though life seems challenging at times, that's only because you're evolving and challenging yourself in the process. It's a good sign.

e. You're focusing more on the long-term rather than the short-term. You're realizing that the long-term benefits of your life are important and need to be addressed now. You're not influenced by short-term needs and gratification any longer. The broader picture is taking shape for you.

f. You don't get angry as often or as easily anymore. You're able to forgive, forget, and move on quicker. You realize that anger is a wasted emotion that has no positive benefits whatsoever. You further realize that the sooner you forgive and move on, the better for your mind and soul. You're not holding on to the past either. As the saying goes, the first to apologize is the bravest, the first to forgive is the strongest, and the first to forget is the happiest.

g.   You trust your intuition more often. Because you believe in yourself and have strong confidence in your decisions and abilities, you find that your intuition is usually right. Your intuition has a greater voice because it comes from a place of strong belief in yourself.

h.   You find yourself easily giving advice to others. You've become a trusted source for others. People are coming to you for advice more frequently. The lives and issues of other people make complete sense to you because you've developed an understanding and empathetic perspective. More importantly, you find yourself wanting to help others.

"The question, 'who am I?' is not meant to get an answer, the question 'who am I?' is meant to dissolve the questioner."

RAMANA MAHARSHI

STAGE 6:

Total Health & Fitness
(The Ultimate Key to Longevity
and Prolonged Life)

No health, no life. It's that simple. Just as life itself is ground zero, your total health and fitness is the ground zero of *your* life, the ultimate driver of the longest possible life you can maximize in your most fit and healthiest physical condition. When you live your life centered on maintaining optimal health, it is extremely possible to live in your best health well into your 90s and 100-plus. This healthy life includes minimal to no prescription drugs, no illnesses, a complete erect posture, strong bones, a strong level of muscle mass, mental sharpness, and mental acuity.

This Stage of your life is rated high on my order of Stages because it goes hand in hand with the complete understanding and acceptance that life is precious. If the only thing you take away from this book is this section on your health and fitness, I will be elated. Once you take your health and fitness seriously on a daily basis to a level that you've never thought possible, all of the other aspects of your life will start to reveal themselves to you. Your entire mind-body-soul connection becomes truly aligned and synchronized. Your health and overall physical and mental well-being are just as significant as all the other aspects of your life. They are integral components in your daily growth quest of understanding, arriving at your true self, and freely living your authentic life. Everything starts with and comes from your health. Without your health, you don't have life.

As I've indicated before, I was truly fortunate to be exposed at a very young age to the world of health and fitness. I was seventeen when my two closest friends invited me to join them after work on their daily workout regimen. The moment I stepped into the gym, all was revealed to me in that instant. I realized with this epiphany that going to the gym was going to be a consistent part of my life forever. I was a skinny, 125-pound, soaking wet high school graduate at that time. I was insecure and lacked confidence because of my very thin body. In that moment however, the world of bodybuilding made me realize that I could literally change and transform my body in any way that I wanted. I thought that if I could transform my physical body, I could also transform my mind. I focused on both intently.

I started going religiously on a daily basis with my friends. They taught me everything about the proper ways of bodybuilding, staying fit, and eating healthy. I was hooked. It was a no-brainer for me. A healthy and ripped body with a healthy mind? Who wouldn't want that? The realizations of gaining weight and muscles, improving my physical appearance, becoming more confident, and living a healthy lifestyle solidified my determination in making this a permanent lifestyle choice. I also learned about the age-defying benefits of working out and being healthy, along with the longevity benefits of living very late into your golden years.

The most immediate and instant benefit you get from working out is the stress that it obliterates out of your body. Working out is one of the best and most effective ways you can manage your stress to a permanent level where it's consistently low or non-existent. For me, going to the gym my entire life on a regular basis has kept my blood pressure in the healthy range my entire life. My blood pressure has literally never been above the normal range. The instant release of stress that happens the moment I step into the gym and lift my first weight is worth its weight in gold. Add to that, listening to my favorite music during my workout, and I feel like I'm lost in my own daily utopia for the 90-120 minutes I'm there. The rest of the world ceases to exist.

The gym is literally the only place in my life where I can routinely unplug from the outside world. I don't mean that in the sense of escapism. I'm a realist living in REALogy®, so I know there's never a way to completely escape. The world is patient and it knows that you'll be coming right back to your problems within a matter of time. What I mean is that not only is the gym my safe haven for two hours, but it is literally the only aspect of my life where I have complete 100% control of literally everything in my environment in those moments. Think about that for a second. In life, there is not one thing where you have complete control. Life doesn't work that way. The minute you wake up in the morning (which is also not in your control), every single thing that you experience that day, life *is in control* of you. You don't have control of your car ride, your job, your friends, how the day goes, literally everything. That's because life is a function of a constant flow of external variables outside of your control. All you have is your control of the perspective you have in all these situations, which is also tricky to manage. The minute things are going great and you're lulled into thinking you have control, bam! There it just went. Something happens to steer you in a different direction. Your perspective and attitude are all you have to make some semblance of the uncontrollability of your life.

When I'm in the gym, I know that I have absolute control and power over every little detail of my workout: how long it is, how heavy I go, how perfect my form is, how hard I push myself, how many reps and sets I do, how much time I choose to waste by talking to people, literally everything. I've flipped the script on life when I'm in the gym because I'm literally deciding everything I'm doing and how I'm doing it. Other than a meteor striking the building, for those two hours of my day, I feel like nothing can stop me and that everything is possible in those moments. That is an incredible feeling of genuine hope that materializes tangibly in the moment. You can actually see hope materializing, transforming you into a very hopeful being. This is one of the many reasons that keeps me coming back to my safe haven of the gym.

Once I learned at a young age that this was to be a permanent fixture in my life, I naturally and logically incorporated it into my life and never deviated from it. As I've previously shared one of my most important philosophies of life: once I know something, I can never un-know it. I will live with that knowledge, and I will put into practice that knowledge as a consistent part of my lifestyle. Any defiance of it will remind me that I'm not living in the truth that I realized and accepted when I became aware of this knowledge. That is the primary self-motivation that keeps me from falling off the wagon.

Since the age of seventeen, I've stayed true to this promise and have consistently maintained my gym-going life on a daily basis. I have stayed healthy, fit, and been in great shape my entire life because of it. The older I get, the more important it is to stay on track. For me, being a gym-lifer from an early age, it has become my religion. Going to the gym is the same as breathing for me. I have to remember to breath to have life. I have to go to the gym to stay healthy and keep that life. If I don't, I will be slowly shorting the length of my maximum life span little by little. I will know it's directly because of a choice I made (or not made).

The health benefits of consistent physical activity into your old age are paramount for maintaining lean muscle mass, strong bones, erect body posture, a healthy mind, and anti-inflammatory disease prevention. In fact, one of my good friends, who's a doctor, has told me that the very first thing doctors learn in medical school is the prevention of diseases and illness, not the treatment and management of such. They are taught that the best medicine for health is consistent exercise as it is naturally and organically preventative. Maintaining strong health as you get older prevents potential illnesses and diseases such as heart disease, various mental diseases and cancers. Additionally, the natural age-defying benefits always keep you looking much younger than your age, with strong skin elasticity, fewer wrinkles, fewer age spots, thinner in the middle, svelte overall appearance, erect posture, and an overall youthful and zesty mental approach to life. You age in years, but you never get old. Staying fit keeps you young, never getting old.

Many of us are not fortunate enough to learn and realize that maintaining health and fitness should be a standard part of our lives, starting at an early age. Consequently, most of us begin to physically decline as we get older, looking and feeling older than our age typically. From birth to about age twenty-five, our bodies are growing into their optimum self. After age twenty-five, our bodies start slowly declining, losing muscle mass, losing bone strength and density, and physically showing the signs of aging. Our DNA strands (the telomeres) start to slowly wither away, which causes the physical manifestation and appearance of aging. However, science has shown and proven that routine physical activity can stave off our natural DNA decline, thereby defying aging and the appearance of getting older.

In its simplest definition, physical activity needs to comprise two basic types of workouts: (1) resistance training that activates your muscles and bones, and (2) cardio activity that stimulates your heart and circulation. Three to six days a week for about sixty to ninety minutes per session are more than sufficient for maintaining a healthy gym routine. The best part is that you can choose any type of muscle resistance training and cardio activity, of which there are infinite choices. You decide the venue and the method as well. You are in complete control in choosing the types of workouts you enjoy so that it doesn't become a burden over time. For example, I enjoy going to the gym, hitting the weights and doing my cardio. My wife enjoys working out at home with plyometric workouts, weight training, and cardio. Whatever your go-to is, you have to not just enjoy it, you have to absolutely love it! Loving it will transform you into a fitness lifer without much effort. You eat the food you love, right? It is the same with your work-out; you will do the ones you love. Working out will become the same as involuntary breathing, where you never have to think about doing it. You just do it automatically. You don't forget to breath, you don't forget to eat and drink, you don't forget to brush your teeth and you won't forget to work out. (These days, I should also add: you don't forget to keep your cell phone glued to your body like an appendage.)

Resistance training can include any type of muscle building, strengthening, and/or maintaining. It can easily be done with weights, cables, resistance bands, your own body weight, etc. Cardio exercises can be done in a variety of ways also, from running, walking, swimming, playing a sport, hiking, etc. Both types of exercise are vital to an overall balanced health and fitness regimen. Muscle resistance training is needed, at a minimum, to offset the loss in muscle mass that naturally occurs as we age. Growing muscle mass is recommended as well. Having good amount of muscle mass keeps you lean and burns calories when resting. Muscle training becomes crucially more important as we age because it prevents bone density loss while strengthening your bones. While you cannot visually see the effects of muscle training in relation to your bone strength, your bones are getting an important life-sustaining benefit internally.

By keeping your bones strong through resistance training, you will prevent the fragile physical body of a much older person who is hunched over and looks weak. Maintaining your bone strength not only will keep your posture erect into your old age, but it will permanently keep away the aid of a walker. It will avoid surgeries and your overall physical decline. You'll be able to continue to use your body in physical ways, such as walking, running and working out. Getting old doesn't mean you have to succumb to its negative effects. You have the control of preventing those negative effects by staying fit and healthy.

While resistance training takes care of your muscles, bones and outward youthful physical appearance, cardio training takes care of the vital internal systems and organs of your heart, lungs, circulation, kidneys, bowels and overall endurance. The combined effects of both workouts also bring with it mental health benefits. Your mind stays sharp, focused, clear, and energized. Your overall and complete mind-body-soul connection ultimately brings you peace of mind and comfort.

More than two-thirds to almost three-fourths of the American population is overweight, with a large majority of that being obese and morbidly obese. This is a staggering number. The Western diet, over the last fifty years in particular, has become so unhealthy that most people are simply just not aware of this fact. Additionally, this diet is infused with high addictive sugars, salts, and saturated fats. The extremely large eating portions have become addictive as well. Many people not only over-eat, but they're eating unhealthy foods most of the time. They're also eating beyond the satisfying point of hunger. Emotional eating has become a problem as well, coupled with consistent nighttime snacking. The stagnant and sedentary lifestyle of many has compounded this problem even further. Consequently, our country has an incredibly high, unacceptable overweight epidemic. When Americans travel abroad, most of the rest of the world can spot us easily, unfortunately by our larger size.

Even though we have amazing modern-day technologies and sciences that have improved and increased our average life span, many obese Americans are dying much sooner and/or looking much older than they are because of this obesity epidemic. All of this can be so easily prevented. The key is for everyone to start learning about health, fitness, and nutrition at a very young age, which I had the accidental fortune of experiencing. When you learn something as a child, it stays with you for life. Health and fitness should be taught in our schools starting in elementary school and continuing through high school. Every year of our education should include a broadened physical education class that is focused on maintaining health, fitness, and proper nutrition. The later years of high school and continuing into the early years of college, this class should also include the hands-on training of students in an actual gym environment. In this way, they learn how to train properly and correctly with the training methods of standard free weights, cables, weight machines, and cardio equipment. We don't just throw our kids into cars and have them start driving, do we? We train them in class. The same should be true for health, fitness, and in-the-gym training.

This concept is so simple and doable. Just like with everything else that children learn at a young age, from school, their parents and their environment, health/fitness/nutrition should be part of the learning process. These are the formative years of a child's life where they learn everything easily, like a sponge dunked in water. By making this part and parcel of a child's early education, imagine how much more informed they will be and how taking care of their bodies becomes a given, not a choice.

When I was exposed to this, I also had the fortune of being properly trained by my experienced friends on how to use the equipment, the type of workouts to perform, how to shift my nutritional habits, and always get the proper amount of sleep for recovery. I wasn't simply thrown into the unknown to learn and fend for myself. During my last thirty-five years of consistently going to the gym, the one common unfortunate thread that I've noticed is that so many people, who know nothing about working out, throw themselves into the gym environment without any knowledge of what to do. What? It's even more unfortunate for the ones who actually think they know what they're doing. While they deserve some credit for taking their bodies to the gym, it is unfortunate that the following simple thoughts haven't occurred to them: (1) they don't know what they're doing and (2) maybe they should get trained first. If you think about it, in the entirety of a person's life, there is literally no scenario, situation, task, job, or endeavor of any kind where that person has NOT received some sort of education, training, or knowledge BEFORE receiving the task. We go to school, we go to college, we are hired at companies who hire us based on our schooling and some level of experience, and we are typically trained to some extent in our jobs, particularly entry-level positions.

How is it possible or even make the slightest sense that a person who has never in their life worked out or had any sort of consistent exercise, simply walks into a gym and starts doing whatever it is that they think they're doing? What's even more nonsensical is that they are potentially causing harm to *their own* bodies without realizing it, instead of creating a perceived health benefit. They falsely believe they are going through the motions of creating a health benefit when in reality they (1) don't realize that they don't know what they're doing and (2) don't know the particular health benefit itself.

They are, at a minimum, not getting any benefit or efficiency from whatever it is they think they're doing, but also potentially putting themselves in harm and injury.

Why, out of all the subjects in the history of mankind on earth, this one subject of health/fitness/working-out is the one and only one for which people do not ever get any training or education, not even on a loose, semi-formal basis? It makes absolutely no sense when you think of it that way, right? Can you imagine applying for a job for which you know that you have no skills, experience, nor knowledge, getting an interview, and the company actually hiring you? Even in the most extreme, slightest chance that you get hired because of your irresistible and magnetic personality (or nepotism), they are still going to TRAIN you first, right? I shake my head every time I see a "newbie" at the gym who clearly doesn't know what they're doing. In those moments, I think about how there should've been some sort of, at least informal education, on this subject matter early in our lives.

If you've never incorporated fitness into your life and you've been inspired by me to do so, my only piece of advice is to start with a trainer. Learn the ropes properly to prevent potential injury from incorrect use of equipment and to be efficient with your time at the gym. Using a trainer will produce results for you much sooner than later, if ever, on your own. But make sure you don't use the trainer as a crutch. The moment you feel like you can take complete control of your fitness, you should do so and drop the trainer, unless you become a fitness competitor or simply desire to take your physical athleticism to an elite level.

Fundamentally, there are three important silos of total health and fitness. They are (1) staying active (i.e., your preferred workout of some type), (2) proper nutrition/eating healthy/proper eating habits, and (3) sleeping the proper amount every night. These are the three pillars of health and fitness, the three sides of a triangle. They each and all must be consistently addressed on a daily basis as part and parcel of your new, long-term healthy lifestyle. It has to become a committed lifestyle, forever! Throw away the idea of temporary dieting and even remove that word from your vocabulary permanently. It's no longer about just losing weight to fit into your summer swimsuit. It's about completely re-programming your brain and your life, to accept that this is your life to be going forward. On this path, you will never have to diet and you will permanently be healthy, fit, and always the size that you want. I've literally never dieted in my life and I've never been overweight in my life. There's no reason for either when you have diligently committed to a healthy lifestyle. When that happens, you simply never have a desire to deviate. It just becomes a permanent, programmed state of mind and physical being, just like breathing. You will have achieved the state of permanent mental transformation through inspiration. When that happens, the physical transformation follows.

In other words, once you have permanently programmed and incorporated a complete and total healthy lifestyle as an involuntary part of your mental and physical existence (akin to the act of involuntary breathing), you're no longer thinking about the requirement of going through the daily acts of healthy living. Now you're just simply doing them without thinking, just like when you breathe without thinking. Consequently, you are always (1) nutritionally sound, (2) staying physically active and fit, and (3) sleeping properly. This then creates a permanent life in which you are rarely overweight (if ever), "dieting" is never in your vocabulary, and you are free (or mostly free) of illnesses and medical concerns. The resulting physical transformation forever remains an integrated part of your life.

Even if you accidentally or purposely deviate on occasion against one (or all) of the three pillars of health and fitness, your body will know and remind you by feeling a bit off. For example, regarding the nutrition pillar, if you're at a social gathering and you're hungry but there is absolutely nothing healthy available, you might eat something that you normally wouldn't, just to satiate the hunger a bit. Because your body is not accustomed to this "foreign" substance, you'll physically feel the slightly-off feeling later that day or the next day. It is your body's reminder, because it always wants to be in homeostasis mode by trending your body back to the accustomed healthy track.

In regards to your preferred workout, if you don't go to the gym for more than the number of days that are typical for you, your body's reminder will be in the form of your mind signaling you pangs of guilt and anxiety for missing workout days. Your lower energy level will be an additional reminder. The combined feelings of guilt, anxiety, and reduced energy will heighten your focus on making sure you hit the gym the very next opportunity, at which point all of these feelings will immediately dissipate. Your body will be thanking you as your mind-body-soul connection becomes aligned again.

Regarding the sleep pillar, your body immediately feels the negative effects the morning after not having slept your normal amount because you stayed up later than typical the night before. A full recovery from sleep has not been met. Your body won't want to wake up at your normal time because it is programmed to get the minimum amount you need. You'll either sleep in to get you there, or you'll start your day feeling off for most of it, especially if you decide not to go to the gym because your body is too tired that morning. Your body is your perfect harbinger when the three sides of the triangle are not aligned. Listening to it is the key.

Following and staying committed to these three sides of the triangle will be challenging if this is your first time making these life-altering changes in your life. However, there is good news. There is a point with your body when the paradigm shift physically and mentally occurs on a permanent basis, beyond the point of no return. In other words, once you stay firmly committed on a daily basis to the routine of working out, eating healthy, and sleeping well, it takes about six months of this consistency for your body to think, "Oh! I see what's happening here!" When that moment comes, your mind and body permanently shift into this new paradigm of living a healthy lifestyle. It becomes normalized. It's now your new norm and your new body. If you start to deviate, it is at this point that your body will remind to get back on track. Prior to this point, your body will fight you to some extent because it wants to go back to the prior accustomed life of unhealthy habits. Remember, that was your life before. Don't be tempted to go back to that life. Once you finally blast through the six-month wall, there's no going back. You're in the clear. It can certainly happen before the six months, or sometime after, but it will happen.

Let's address all three sides of the triangle in more detail. As mentioned before, it is imperative that you find the type of workout that you like and enjoy, one that fits your life and time-management. When you always come back to something you enjoy and love, it won't feel over-bearing. I realize that the biggest hurdle to working out is finding the time. I also know that you probably make time for everything else in your life that you feel is important, right? This is more important than some of your other things, because this is your life after all, and certainly important enough to create the time for your health maintenance and optimization. In the worst-case scenario, if you're extremely busy and time becomes an issue, commit yourself to waking up an hour early three to four times per week; it doesn't have to be every day. That will be sufficient. The morning is always the best time to work out anyway. The mix of your workout should be thirty to forty minutes of muscle resistance training and twenty to forty minutes of cardio training. If you have to split up the two types of workouts during the day because of time issues or because of the location of each type of workout, then that's fine. For example, you may like to run in the mornings in your neighborhood and then later in the day go to the gym to hit the weights.

Proper nutrition includes eating healthy (the right foods in the right amounts) and having good eating habits. This will be challenging if you're coming from a place of consistent over-eating and poor eating habits. It may take more time to master this pillar than the other two because this area has more psychology entrenched as part of the challenge. The strongest advice I can give to break the psychological hold of prior bad habits is to start with small steps by scaling back initially instead of a complete overhaul. You also should remind yourself every morning of the commitment you've made to yourself to change. You have to consistently remind yourself that you've made a significant emotional and psychological choice in your life to permanently change your life. If that choice also happens to be a function of an illness or a required surgery that was created by your prior habits, then let that serve as a Significant Emotional Event in your life. Sometimes, we go through either life-altering or perhaps what could have been life-ending experiences in our lives such as cardiac arrest, strokes, heart surgery, cancer, etc. I refer to these experiences as Significant Emotional Events. Sadly, sometimes the occurrence of such an event is what forces a person to permanently commit to finally making a change in their life.

I would also suggest that if you live with a partner, that partner has to fully commit to understanding you and supporting you during this process. Ideally, if the partner can do it with you, it will be better for the both of you.

Proper nutrition means (1) learning and understanding the portions and calories you should be eating in a day, (2) learning the proper mix of proteins, fats, and carbohydrates, and (3) improving your overall eating habits. If weight loss is the initial concern, drastically reducing your caloric intake is the first step. If you've been eating over 3,000 calories per day and you're overweight, you have to start eating less than 3,000 calories per day. I would suggest a small breakfast, small lunch, normal dinner, and healthy snacks between lunch and dinner, if you feel you need it.

You should either completely eliminate or significantly reduce the following from your daily diet: …(1) sugars, particularly refined sugars, (2) salts/sodium, (3) processed foods, (4) alcohol (these are empty calories), (5) junk food, (6) all fast foods (think of McDonald's as the devil), (7) all sodas, and (8) any foods high in saturated fats or too high in carbohydrates. You can have sweets as a reward or on occasion in small portions, but try to significantly reduce them from your diet. Proteins should comprise 40% to 70% percent, carbohydrates 20% to 30% and healthy fats (directly from the source) 10% to 25%. Good proteins are fish, chicken, lean meats, beans, and vegetables. Good carbohydrates are complex carbohydrates from vegetables. Avoid or reduce starch-based carbohydrates like pasta. Good fats are various proteins, nuts, oils, and some vegetables. The minimal types of supplements I would suggest along with your food intake is a multi-vitamin, Vitamin D, and Omega 3. If weight loss is the initial goal, losing one to two pounds per week is a good, steady, and balanced trend for weight loss. Don't focus on the time it takes to get you to your desired weight loss goal. Slow and steady is the healthiest form of weight loss. It is the most effective and long-lasting. You never want to lose weight on a crash basis.

Another important note on weight loss is don't focus on the weight itself, meaning don't worry about your starting weight and your desired ending weight. Throw the thought of numbers in pounds out of your head. Focus on reducing your body fat percentage in relation to your muscle mass percentage. The goal is to increase your muscle mass through resistance training, thereby reducing your body fat as a result, through proper nutrition and cardio. In other words, if your body fat percentage is too high, focus on reducing it over time to its proper level. For women, a great athletic range is 18% to 25% and a good range is up to 32%. For men, a great athletic range is 8% to 12% and a good range is up to 19%.

For women, focus more on how much better your clothes start fitting you and that your body is contouring the way you want. Your weight in terms of the number in pounds is no longer relevant, especially if strength training is part of your consistent routine. Your higher muscle mass and your lower body fat percentage do not necessarily translate to a drop in weight, nor should it. Dropping dress sizes is better than focusing on the drop in actual weight. Don't concern yourself with body mass index (BMI) either. It's a misnomer if you are consistently working out with a proper mix of muscle building and cardio. It will indicate an erroneous high value because it only takes your height and weight into account, without accounting for heavier weighing muscle mass. The most important barometers are body fat and muscle mass percentages.

Again, I know that losing weight and changing your nutritional habits are the hardest things you will ever do. I understand that. It's much easier said than done. Changing your perspective on what eating really means is the main key to successfully breaking your bad habits. In other words, you literally need to change the paradigm in your mind of what proper eating is and destroy what you've learned about eating to that point. Here's what I mean. When I learned at a young age that eating right and staying fit were absolutely essential to healthy living, I truly chose to look at food differently from that point on. Food became to me as nothing more than nutritional sustenance to give me a healthy life. I began to eat for nutrition, not for pleasure. Although I certainly enjoy what I eat and savor every taste, I look at food as simply proteins, carbs, and fats. I eat because I know that my body needs these three essential macros along with vitamins and minerals. I keep nutrition top of mind instead of the act itself. This helps me to remember that I only need a certain portion at a time to (1) satisfy my hunger and (2) attain the necessary amount of the macros, vitamins, and minerals. More than that would be over-eating. Once this type of thought process becomes permanently programmed, then there's never any other way that you view food.

Another way to make the shift in your mind on eating is to focus on the very act itself. In other words, visualize and become acutely aware of the extremely short physical act of raising a fork to your mouth. It takes about a second to raise a fork/spoon/your hand to your mouth. If you pause that second and actually look at the item of food that is a second away of entering your mouth, you are able to decide in that second if that item of food will help your body, or if it will hurt your body. Pause and actually look at the food you're about to insert in your mouth. Once that item goes into your mouth, that's it. It is forever gone and permanently ingested into your body to be digested. Once digested, will your body extract the positive benefits of that food item? Or will there be a detrimental effect to your body? There is no turning back or changing your mind on what you just swallowed. You have to live with that decision forever.

If you believe your life to be precious and that you only get one life, why would you knowingly place an item of food (or drink) in your mouth that you know to be unhealthy for you? The actual physical act of pausing while you're eating, to confirm that you're eating something good for you, will make you truly think more often about what's actually going in your body. This practice will make it easier for you over time to avoid the unhealthy foods that you know to be as such. It won't be a matter of guilt any longer, just simply a matter of the correct choice that won't require much thought any more. There's no decision making needed any longer. You'll know the right from the wrong, the healthy from the unhealthy.

Let me give you one final way of thinking about it, albeit, prepare yourself because some might find this disgusting. It is the same image I used previously; I have to use a very drastic type of metaphor to prove my simple point. If I were to ask you to pick up the corpse of a dead rat in an alley and take a bite out of it, just the image alone will make you recoil in convulsion. You couldn't even imagine doing such a disgusting thing, let alone thinking about the toxins and poisons that exist in that corpse. Well, the same is true for every type of unhealthy food that you place in your mouth. You may not be consciously aware of the high saturated fat content or any other negative aspect of it in that moment, but over time, the accumulation of these toxins from these foods will adversely affect your health. If you start thinking of every unhealthy type of food in this matter, you'll stop eating such foods soon enough.

When it comes to the third pillar of sleep, this is the most underrated aspect of fostering and maintaining proper health. Many people do not realize that the proper amount of sleep is not only needed for many recovery purposes, but it is a great anti-aging aspect of your routine. The correct amount of sleep on a daily basis properly rejuvenates your body by allowing the adequate time that is needed for every single new cell of your body to be formed. Proper sleep not only rejuvenates your body, but also your mind. You wake up clearheaded, energized, and ready to take on the day. This consistency contributes to a healthy mental state as well. Personally, I really enjoy my sleep. I love sleep. I'm a big fan of sleep. I love to take naps as well when I have a few moments. Sleep for me is an easily controllable aspect of my life where I know that as long as I do it, I'm tremendously contributing to the long-term positive health of my life. Many people, particularly young people, take sleep for granted. Just as proper amount of sleep has many benefits, the consistent lack of it has negative effects as well. Your mental state starts to suffer, your body feels week and fatigued, and you lack the energy and drive to be productive. Over time, the lack of sleep can result in illnesses, high levels of stress and anxiety, high blood pressure, and possible strokes and cardiac arrest.

I cannot stress enough the importance of a scaled balance of consistent physical activity, proper nutrition, and the right amount of sleep every night. When you've mastered this consistency and aspect of your life, you truly feel that your mind, body, and spirit are always in line and strongly connected to each other. This is vital in your quest to live freely in your authentic life. When you don't feel in sync with every aspect of your life, it doesn't afford you the time and headspace that you need to think beyond the everyday aspects of life. Your total health, fitness level, and nutrition keep you aligned and connected. It all starts with the physical care of your body so that your mind can be at peace to then sync up with your body and spirit.

Start taking care of yourself today. Don't wait to make it a New Year's resolution for example. We should be celebrating every new day, week, and month, not just every new year. Making a resolution at the beginning of the year is a huge fallacy. It's a time waster. It is fleeting and a huge cop-out. You should be making resolutions every day of your life based on everything you learn about bettering yourself along the way. That's how you consistently improve. Make a permanent resolution now to commit to the three-prong approach to living your best and healthiest life. After all, what do most highly successful people have in common? They don't waste time. They place a high importance on their healthy lifestyle by making time for exercise, by eating well, and by getting the proper amount of sleep to stay productive and successful. This cycle of life constantly serves as fuel for their success.

"He who has health, has hope; and he who has hope, has everything."

ARABIAN PROVERB

STAGE 7:

Total Life Fitness
(Daily Life Enhancement Goals)

Is your life fit? Have you ever considered your life being fit, or in terms of your overall life fitness? Just as health and fitness should be a daily pursuit, so should the fitness of your life. The word "workout" should now embody two types: (1) your body workout for your health and (2) your daily life enhancement workout, for your life fitness.

What I mean by that is you should objectively and consciously live your daily life by making enhancements in your life to maintain the fitness of it. On your lifelong journey of personal growth, making sure that your life is fit and that you are in a constant state of enhancing and improving it is the biggest aspect of this growth. Now that you've harnessed the power of your mind, transcended beyond your personal history, and incorporated daily health and fitness into your life, developing a mindset of life fitness as a daily endeavor becomes an easy next step.

This daily pursuit and process is important because it not only re-enforces your life's journey of growth, but it keeps you grounded on a daily basis by monitoring this ascension. It also helps serve as a habitual support system in times of self-doubt, sense of rejection, experiencing failures, or loss of confidence. When you have a plan and a program that you are following every day, one that is thought out, written, and self-monitored, it forces you to follow it. It also brings you back to center when you feel like you're a little overwhelmed with too much going on in your life.

The ultimate objective is to make life fitness an ingrained daily routine of your life, whereby you are automatically and involuntarily going through the required steps without having to think about it. Just like health and fitness have become as easy as breathing for you, your life fitness embraces this same metaphor. You have to devote time to your life fitness workout as you would to your body workout routine.

The good news is that the amount of time you need to devote to life fitness is about ten minutes in the evening and ten minutes in the morning. So not long at all, it is very doable and achievable. Most importantly, it can easily become a daily routine. There are simple ways this can be achieved on a daily basis. The process of incorporating life enhancements into your program every day has to do with setting daily goals, not short-term or long-term goals, but just daily goals. These are goals that have to be completed in one day.

Here is what I mean. You will still need to know and plan for any goals that take longer than one day to complete, such as your short-term and long-term goals in the broader sense. Short-term and long-term goals are clearly integral to your overall growth objective and life fitness. However, the principal difference is that they will now be incorporated in your daily goals so that you're monitoring and tracking your long-range goals on a daily basis as you're simultaneously completing *all* the daily goals.

So here is the simple process of incorporating life enhancements through daily goals.

1. Every evening before you go to sleep, take about ten minutes, or as little or as much amount of time you may need, to list approximately three to five tasks/goals that you definitely want to check off your list and accomplish the next day. Every evening, you will be writing down, in order of importance, all the goals you wish to accomplish and complete the next day.

2. You can list as many goals as you want that you believe you can definitely complete the next day.

3. These goals will include task-oriented objectives that need to be completed both in your personal and professional lives. But they will also include broader goals in the greater scheme of incorporating life enhancements to make you a better person that next day. The task-oriented objectives will naturally make you a better person as well.

4. Here is the most important part. Assuming you have a separate list (which is the recommended method) of your short-term goals and long-term goals that require longer than a day to complete, or you are firmly aware of what they are (without a list), include specifically detailed tasks and goals on this daily list that can be and should be completed the next day in service of these long-range goals. In other words, you are routinely and habitually working on your long-term goals on a daily basis, without fail.

5. The next important step is not to feel the need or burden to include as many goals as possible. In fact, it is quite the oppo-

site. You need to make the accomplishment and completion of these goals for the very next day as realistic and feasible as possible. In other words, don't make a goal that you know requires an uncontrollable third-party's response that will take several days for that response. Also, as it pertains to the daily pursuit of the longer ranged goals, the same principle applies. Do not feel the need to accomplish them as soon as possible. The key is that you're continuing to take the needed steps on a daily basis, regardless of how many days it will take. Taking steps is the most important action, one step at a time.

6. Keep the written information by your bedside. Once you've compiled your list of goals specifically for the next day, review them in your mind as you're trailing off to sleep. Visualize them in the writing you just made and visualize your next day's pursuit of them. In other words, you are visualizing the goals themselves and visualizing your actions the next day in completion of these goals.

7. As you're reviewing and visualizing in your mind, you may realize you have to make adjustments. Since you have the information right next to your bed, make the changes quickly so you don't forget them before trailing off to sleep. The review and visualization process will actually help you fall asleep, but only if you're doing so in an exciting, anticipatory manner in which you can't wait to hit those goals the next day. If you're feeling anxious and overwhelmed, that will keep you from falling asleep. Change your goals so as to put your mind at ease. Sleep is vital, so don't ruin it by keeping your mind from being at ease and rested.

8. When you wake up in the morning, incorporate the ten minutes you need to review your list of life enhancements. This should

be part of your normal morning routine. Make this an ingrained habit, without fail.

9. During your morning review, you are accomplishing two things: (1) making any additional final changes and (2) getting you mentally prepared for the day's performance.

10. You will find that the morning review will bring you more clarity and awareness of the goals. You will realize that what you thought the prior evening is not necessarily realistic or maybe no longer needed for this particular day. What happens sometimes is that the night before, we feel invincible and want to bite off more than we can chew. The morning brings us back to reality and gives us the clarity needed to make realistic adjustments.

11. In fact, in that ten-minute morning review, you might check off one or two of the goals right then and there as you realize the necessary realistic adjustments that need to be made.

12. When your day is complete, hopefully you will have accomplished every single goal on that list. If not, that's ok. It's going to take a few days, maybe weeks to really master the art of making realistic life enhancement goals on a daily basis.

13. Remember that this is a daily planning and accomplishing objective. This is not a daily accumulation of goals that will be completed in the future. They have to be completed that day. That's how you become better from these accomplished life enhancements.

14. Make a new list of enhancements that evening before going to bed for the next day to complete. Again, these goals should include both your daily tasks and tasks that can be completed the following day in pursuit of the long-range goals.

15. Before you know it, not only are you growing on a daily basis and therefore improving your overall life fitness, but you're also checking off your long-term goals one by one from the accumulated effect of the prior days' accomplishments.

For example, a task-oriented goal might be: follow-up with my clients to make sure all their needs have been addressed. A broader life enhancement goal might be: make sure I read two articles today that address ways of achieving personal growth. Both of these types of goals can be completed in one day and the same day. And both of them provide learning lessons that help you become a better person. Following up with clients helps you listen to their concerns and address them in a positive manner from an empathetic perspective. Reading the articles improves your knowledge and emotional intelligence. An example of a daily goal in pursuit of a long-term goal might be: share something meaningful on social media that helps you professionally in your business or career. This daily goal helps in the pursuit of your long-term goal of increasing your number of followers to a certain amount for business purposes.

Having a daily routine, seven days a week, that specifically focuses on improving your life fitness not only accomplishes the feat in question, but it truly gives you a daily sense of purpose. This purpose serves as reinforcement that keeps you on track. Once it becomes an involuntary routine in your life, you feel proud and really good about yourself because you know that improving yourself is now an effortless task. It doesn't feel like you have to work on it any longer. It just happens. This further keeps the fuel of your confidence always burning.

You've self-inspired yourself into a new routine that has become a permanent staple in your life. When you go about your day accomplishing what you've set to accomplish, you go to bed that night feeling that you were completely productive that day, without having wasted any time of your life during that period. When these productive days consistently turn into productive weeks, months, and years, you start feeling like the most accomplished person. Your sense of purpose, meaning, and growth all align together. That alignment keeps you focused, confident, determined, and committed to everything that you know you are capable of achieving.

"You must do the things you think you cannot do."

ELEANOR ROOSEVELT

STAGE 8:

Your Human Relationships

Where would you be without your relationships, particularly the one with yourself? A relationship is the life-blood for human existence and survival. As social human beings, we are conditioned to create and maintain connections with other people. These connections are the blood flow that keeps us linked and gives us reasons and meaning for existing and living. Without these connected links, we will ultimately perish because the reason to exist goes away. Even in the rare case of a person who has chosen a permanent life of solitude, that person has at least one special relationship that keeps him going, an unbreakable bond of a relationship with himself, and possibly with a loyal faith in a higher spiritual existence.

The entirety of Live in the REAL! is centered on the relationship with yourself, first and foremost. To improve upon and elevate this self-relationship, Stage 8 is largely focused on your inter-personal relationships with your family, friends, colleagues, followers, and all of humanity. These significant inter-personal relationships are sacred. They should always be nurtured, protected, and broadened, which in turn, cultivate your self-relationship.

Your closest relationships with your family and inner circle of friends serve as your reliable support system and are vital for your continued growth and success. As with many areas of our lives that are reliable and consistently available, we take our relationships for granted and lose focus of the importance of these relationships. We forget to nurture and protect our relationships, yet we habitually turn to them in our moment of need. We tend to place ourselves ahead of the people on the other side of the relationship and the relationship itself. This happens because most people don't realize that just as in other aspects of our lives that require hard work and attention, relationships are organic entities that require hard work and attention as well.

Your Significant Partner Relationship

The most easily forgotten and unattended relationship is our spouse or significant partner in our lives. This occurs because we get so busy with working hard and diligently in other areas of our lives, that it becomes easy to place our partner on the back burner. We work so hard on our education, our careers, our various obligations, etc. that we run out of time to work on our relationship with our most significant right-hand person. We don't include the necessary time for the work required in our relationship because we maintain the presumptive thought process that (1) our partner will always be there for us, (2) that it's their job to be there for us, and (3) that there's always time to focus on our partner — the I'll-get-to-it-tomorrow mentality.

Marriage or any equivalent long-term committed relationship REQUIRES hard work just as much, if not more, than the other important areas of your life. It is vital that not only you accept this reality, but that you truly understand what it means and that you genuinely incorporate this understanding in your day-to-day living patterns. Most people enter into marriage not aware of this crucial component, so naturally they are ultimately bound to fail. Others, who do know but choose to forget it, follow the same inevitable course. Both parties need to be fully aware at the beginning of marriage that it is an organic being that requires attention, love, and hard work to keep it alive. There are no short cuts to love. And lasting love requires hard work.

When you don't work on your relationship, you become slowly disconnected. You start to grow in different directions. You start leading separate paths that ultimately culminate in what feels like inevitable divorce. You get to the point where you firmly believe that your relationship is permanently broken and unsalvageable because you never gave yourself any opportunity along the way to re-route this path. Sadly, most divorces could have been prevented. Any time devoted to work could have re-directed the course. Partners simply need to be reminded that the spark is still there, that they are still in love with each. But the layers of disconnection and separate paths that have formed due to years of inattention bury the spark and love so deeply, that people are too overwhelmed by the process of reconciliation and salvaging.

What does it mean to "work" on a relationship? It means the following bullet points.

a.   Remind yourself that you don't *need* each other. You should *want* each other. Treat your marriage/commitment as your first child before having your first child. You have to care, love, and nurture that child of commitment every day. You cannot love selfishly where you're on the receiving end without equal reciprocation. Further, your love is to be given away unselfishly to your partner.

b.   Become aware, truly understand, and firmly believe that a relationship is organic, fluid, and growing. It requires continued and consistent love and attention as food for survival.

c.   Your partner is the most important person and co-pilot in your life each and every day of your life. Equally the same is true that you're the most important person in your partner's life. That being the case, how and why could you possibly take each for granted? It doesn't make sense logically, right? How is it possible to forget who's the most important person in your life?

d.   If your relationship didn't originally start out as a friendship, try to create one as early as possible in the relationship. View each other as not just romantic partners, but also as life-long best friends to each other. Talk to each other as friends would, care for each other as friends would, and help and support each other as friends would. This is an added dimension of loving and caring for one another. My wife and I, for example, started as friends before dating. Once married, I've considered my wife as my best friend and likewise for her.

e.   Always have genuine and real discussions and communication. Communicate beyond the superficial level. Dig deeper. Go beyond the daily bullet points of the grind of life. Ask questions of one another and listen intently to the answers. Believe the answers as well, and take them to heart.

f.   Listen to each other intently. Don't interrupt the other person when talking. Let them complete their thoughts, even if it takes a while. Don't be hesitant to share uncomfortable subjects. Plow through it. Your partner will appreciate and thank you for it. If your partner isn't the one with whom you can share your most sensitive thoughts, then who is?

g.   Create a genuine understanding that each person is free to bring up a disagreement or complaint about you at any time. There's no need to ignore it or deny it. As difficult as it might be, listen to your partner's complaint about you objectively without interruption. Acknowledge their concern first, before you respond.

h.   When fighting and arguing, try to remember that you're still each other's best friend and most important person to each other. This is the most difficult aspect of a relationship. It's almost impossible to keep a cooler head. Emotions have taken over, not to mention, one or both partners feeling resentment, hurt, lack of support, and/or betrayal of trust. As difficult as it may be, try not to use insulting words that you'll regret later. Insults, judgments, and judgmental phrases serve no purpose at all. In fact, they make the arguments worse. Try to stay on the subject matter as much as possible and as objectively as possible. If it gets too heated, you may have to pause to cool down. If you're not able to resolve the argument in the moment or later in the day, try with all your might to resolve it by the next day. It's not a good idea for an argument to last more than a day. The more you practice this habit, the easier it will become.

i.   The most difficult hurdle to overcome when fighting/arguing with your partner is the built-in defense systems that kick-in and blind you to the reality of the situation and to the core of the issues being argued. In addition to each person becoming instantly defensive, there are argument patterns and behaviors that each person has been accustomed to over time when arguing with their long-time partner, which further blind each other to the crux of the matter. In other words, the "here we go again" mentality kicks in and each fighter goes into his/her neutral corner to come out fighting from a position of defensiveness and typical arguing behavior. Instead of actually hearing and listening to each other, the combined effects of the defense mechanisms and pre-disposed argument patterns completely escalate the argument with no end in sight. No one is being heard, and more importantly, the issue is not really being addressed. Each person continues to make the wrong assumptions (because of and as a function of prior arguments) about the other person and doesn't take the time to realize that (1) a fair point is being made, (2) someone might actually be wrong, and (3) usually both are wrong to some extent. Certainly no one likes to admit when they're wrong. The "boy who cried wolf" mentality (because of the arguing pattern precedent on each part) prevents one partner from truly listening to the other to understand the actual issue. As difficult as it is, you must remember to defy your instinctual patterns and behaviors of arguing and refrain as much as possible from taking on a defensive position and arguing in your habitual manner. You must pause and try as hard as possible to listen to and hear the legitimate issue of your partner so it can finally be addressed constructively. Lastly, it is important that apologies and admissions when wrong are made, as difficult as it may be. The more you do so, the more you realize you start to argue less, and that future arguments become much shorter because each person is finally being heard.

j.   Most often, the underlying causes and reasons for a hard-wired defense mechanism when arguing with a partner stem from years of unresolved issues and various prior traumas that a person carries with them into a relationship. These unresolved issues and traumas manifest from all phases of life including childhood, teenage years, and early adulthood. They are also a function of negative experiences from any and all human contact points in a person's life including parents, siblings, friends, teachers, co-workers, prior relationship partners, and overall environmental and societal contacts. All of these latent, unresolved, unaware, and un-analyzed issues and traumas are thrust upon your current partner in your current relationship. The most important and simplest approach to lessen the severity of arguments and reduce the frequency of them is to remember not to victimize and blame your partner for your own history, during which your partner did not exist. Your partner should not be made an innocent target. Secondly, although we haven't yet started to work on resolving our past issues, at a minimum, we need to (1) acknowledge their existence and (2) understand that they may be the cause of strife and conflict in our current relationship. These understandings will at least pave the way for starting the healing process in your current relationship, short of ultimately following through with needed therapy.

k. Date each other regularly. Go out once or twice a month. Go on vacations with each other. Have genuine fun with each other. Dating should be an absolute must and regularity in the relationship. Don't forget to be boyfriend and girlfriend to each other, not just husband and wife. My wife and I refer to our dates and vacations as B&G time, meaning boyfriend and girlfriend time. We pretend and act like we're not married, that we're still dating each other. B&G time is a must! It leads to more frequent unselfish love making, with quality and meaningful intimacy, which leads to a stronger connection. This consistent connection is what forms an unbreakable bond.

l. If you're fairly compatible with each, doing things together is not difficult. Plan the time to do so. If you're not as compatible, find the areas of common ground and common interests and do them together regularly. Plan the time to do so.

m. If you don't feel and believe that during every minute of your relationship you can be your true self at all times, then you have to work on getting there. Your partner is the one person in your life that you should feel free to be your true self 24/7. The best way to get there is to start sharing more about yourself with your partner. Before you know it, you'll realize that you've stopped "acting" around your partner, that you're just being yourself without trying. That is a very refreshing and liberating feeling. I'm always being the goofy, silly, funny, idiotic person that I am around my wife, because I know I can. And even though I know it annoys her at times, I know that she has no problem with me simply being myself.

n. Sit on the couch together, not apart. Always stay within touching range of each. Try to watch programs together, not apart. It's okay to have your own programs that the other doesn't watch. But for the most part, when together in the house, try to watch programs together as often as possible. If there are other different things you like to do, try to do them at the same time in the same room together. Physical proximity is always essential.

o. Do mundane daily things together as well. Go Costco shopping together, get gas together, and run errands together. It doesn't have to be all the time, but sometimes would be nice.

p. Have a clear understanding of each other's household responsibilities. Help each other with those responsibilities even if it's not one of yours. If you're free and available, helping your partner is always appreciated.

q. Hug each other often. Hugging releases endorphins, making you instantly feel better and comforted. Touch each other frequently. Hello and goodbye kisses are a must as well.

Non-sexual touching keeps the connection intact and is a quick non-verbal signal that you're thinking of each other.

Not everything will run smoothly even when you're trying your genuine best. But the most important point is that you're aware of these work items and that you're truly working on the relationship on a daily basis. Remember that while you don't have a choice in who your family members are, you do with your partner. You're the one who chose your partner, so remember to cherish this person on a daily basis as the most important person in your life without exception.

The Relationship with Your Children

When it comes to your relationship with your child(ren), this relationship is truly unlike any other. While unconditional love would be an ideal achievement for every relationship in your life (particularly in a marriage/life partnership), the relationship with your children is the closest to unconditional love as you can get, if not fully there for many parents. The cliché that "I would do anything for my children" is true for many parents. The fact that you literally brought life to your kids is indescribable, which is why you hold these relationships most dear to you. These relationships literally last a lifetime and you never stop thinking about them as your kids no matter their age.

However, even though we probably have the most love for our children than anyone else, no amount of love can replace the effort that it takes to maintain a wonderful and healthy relationship with your children. The younger they are the easier it is for us to control the relationship to our liking. Once they get older and start forming confident personalities, our relationship transforms into one that has to be more compromising to take their feelings and positions into account. This is where and when it becomes difficult for parents to start letting go of some of that control they've had. Our love and concern for our kids strongly influence our desire to maintain as much control as possible. As late teenagers and young adults, they start to fight this control and try to pull it in their favor. The delicate line between allowing our children to make their own decisions as they become young adults versus how much influence we have over their decisions becomes more challenging to balance. During this time, we must remain confident and have faith that the decision-making and problem-solving skills that we have imparted onto them will guide them properly in their own paths.

Our relationship with our children is fraught with many challenges, at the core of which is the delicate balance of letting them live their own individualized lives while still having some semblance of influence and control. If not managed carefully and gingerly, our children may begin to resist our interpretation of this delicate balance. This relationship can be further complicated if the parents are divorced and sharing custody. Additionally, if and when step-parents enter into the children's lives, maintaining your own relationship with your children has now become a bit more challenging. There are many delicate balances that now have to be considered.

Regardless of the total parenting involved in your children's lives above and beyond your own, it is vital that you maintain a special and strong-linked relationship with them. The younger your children are when divorce and/or additional parents become involved the more crucial and life-dependent it is that you establish and maintain an unbreakable bond with your children as early in their lives as possible. With the challenges of being separated/divorced, it is vitally imperative that you also create and maintain viable relationships with your ex-partner and/or a step-parent, in which honest communication, trust, and mutual respect across all parties are of paramount importance. Your successful long-term relationship with your children also greatly depends on the positive and healthy ones you maintain with all concerned parties (including ex-parents-in-law).

A healthy and successful relationship with your children means that you are involved in their lives in an immersive way and are directly connected to them on a daily basis. That involvement and connection has to be in ways where your children never hesitate to contact you at a moment's notice for any reason at all, big or small. They have to know that you will drop everything when needed by them. They should know this to be the case without ever doubting themselves about reaching out to you. Your unconditional availability to them should be an absolutely given and normal aspect of their lives that they never think twice about. There should never be a moment that your children feel that you are not available to them. You are their ultimate support system, security, protection, guidance, discipline, cheerleader, and literally everything else in their lives, so there is no reason that they should be in a position to ever doubt that.

When you are with your children, you should be present in those moments. They need to know and feel that you value their time. You should be actively listening to their stories, hopes, and aspirations. Your encouragement of their imagination, creativity, and ideas means the world to them. You need to also consistently model in yourself the adults that you want them to become. When such strong relationships are formed and cultivated at a young age, it makes for their transition into adulthood much easier because they grow up with the much needed love, support, and encouragement on a consistent basis.

At the same, the transition of your relationship with them from children to adults also becomes easier. The level of mutual respect remains very high as the relationship into their adulthood grows stronger. Once your children are adults, the same levels of support, love, and guidance should continue. The only difference now is that they are fully living their own lives on their own without your daily monitoring. But the high level of support and encouragement should not change. They may not admit it as adults, but they appreciate and continue to feel good about having this support. Family is everything and is always your top priority.

My Father-Daughters Relationships

Since I'm a father of three amazing daughters who are now in their twenties, I must comment on the raising of daughters and the extreme significance of a strong father-daughter relationship. A woman's life is made a little easier to navigate when raised by loving parents and also one in which her father is a constant active participant in her life. It is not enough for a father to simply be present. A father has to show tremendous amount of love and support on a consistent daily basis. I made certain that the minute each of my three daughters was born, that I would smother them with love, affection, hugs, and kisses on a daily basis. I would tell them how much I love them, how proud I am, and how intelligent and strong they are.

A consistent and routine hug and "I love you" go a long way in the development of a young girl, and not just exhibited on special occasions. You should be showing love and sharing hugs on a consistent daily basis. A combination of being told and shown how much you love them and are proud of them in their formative years helps them develop into tremendously strong and confident young women. From a very young age, I've instilled, demonstrated, and taught my daughters that they should be nothing less than internally bad-ass, strong-willed, fully confident young woman who have no chink in their armor. At the same time however, this strength is balanced with being kind-hearted, extremely humble, and caring women who value and respect others. My symbol for them (and myself for that matter) that exemplifies this philosophy is the elephant.

An elephant is a wondrous, beautiful creature who displays tremendous strength and fortitude physically, but is the most kind, sensitive, humble being internally, one that cares and values its family members and other elephants above himself. But don't mistake that kindness for weakness, for an elephant (and my daughters) will charge at you when even mildly disrespected. I'm proud to say that all three of my daughters are elephants. They all have amazing strength, confidence, and clear visions of their identities. But they also have the kindest hearts that my wife and I have fostered.

Confidence is a fragile concept. It's easy to lose it and/or difficult to develop. But once the switch of full awareness and realization is made in your mind, you can instantly become the most confident person in the world, the kind of confidence that stays with you for a lifetime. When a father outwardly exhibits love, support, pride, and encouragement on a consistent basis to his daughter, that switch in the daughter's mind becomes very clear and ever-present. All she has to do is tap into it and flip the switch. Once the switch is flipped, there's no going backwards, especially when you continue to have the loving support of your parents, one that includes a strong father-daughter relationship. That confidence helps them make better dating decisions, education decisions, and career decisions. As a father, I don't have to worry about all their life decisions that they're making on their own as strong and driven young women.

Even though my daughters are adults now, I still give those hugs and kisses (much less than when they were children) and continue to exhibit my love and pride for them. My daughters know that they will always have me in their lives no matter what. I can see how just that support alone helps them strive for everything that they want for themselves. I can see how they are following their passions and visions, much more so than I ever did as a young man.

I can't speak to a father-son relationship since I haven't had that good fortune, but I can say that mothers are typically much more ever-present and consistently active in their children's lives, so I would venture to guess that a mother's relationship with her son is usually a strong one as well. While young men typically do not always need an outward display of love, a mother will usually provide that anyway and will always, at a minimum, provide consistent love, support, and encouragement. A healthy father-son relationship is also extremely important. A good father's model for their son makes a difference in the type of young man a son becomes. Young men tend to model their fathers more so in their younger years before becoming young adults, so it is vitally important to have a strong model for a father.

It's important to note that my parenting advice applies to both married parents and divorced. In the case of the latter, the major difference is that each parent has to try a little harder to foster and maintain their relationships with their children since they don't have the advantage of all living together under the same roof. And by all means, please do not EVER use the excuse of being divorced to explain why you don't have the same relationship with your child. You just have to try harder in making that relationship the number one priority in your life. In fact, it is imperative that children of divorced parents continue to have strong relationships with each parent. As a divorced parent, you have to keep your child's well-being above and beyond any difficult situation you may have resulting from the divorce. Never use divorce as an excuse because it's a cop-out.

Your Friend Relationships

Your friend relationships are different and unique from all others. They will change over your lifetime. You have childhood friends that remain lifelong friends and you have new friends that you meet along the way. You lose friends, you gain friends. You break up with friends. You have friends that sadly pass away. You know your real friends from your casual friends. The common theme among all your friends is that you get to choose each and every one of them.

The friend relationship is special. When you have one or two close ones that you consider your best friends, they are a needed and vital support system beyond your family. Many times in your life, this special friend is there for you in times when you need to confide in someone that isn't your significant partner or family member. It is very therapeutic to have such friends. From a psychological perspective, we feel more comfortable and assured that we have people in our lives that we've chosen to have in our lives, in addition to our direct family. It gives us a subliminal sense of balance and psychological equilibrium.

For me personally, I've always been a bit of a loner. I've purposely only had one or two best friends in my life. In fact, one is my wife and one is a male friend that I've known longer than my wife. As I look back in my life, I've noticed that I've purposely chosen not to befriend too many people in my life. Because of my private nature, I've been able to see who the "real" people are as opposed to "fake" friends. I've stayed away from "fake" friends. Honestly, once I married my soul mate, I've never felt the need to have any additional close friends. You may have many friends, and many close friends for that matter. My only suggestion and piece of advice would be to make sure that the people you keep close to you are "real", in the sense that they truly care about you. When you have a friend that you know will unconditionally accept you for who you are, that is the friend you want. A friend that you know will take a bullet for you is the keeper. But likewise, you also accept this friend unconditionally and will take a bullet for him/her as well. This is a friend for life. This is the relationship you need to nurture and care for on a consistent basis. This is the brother or sister that you have *chosen* to be in your life.

Your Family Relationship: Parents, Siblings, Cousins, Extended Family

This is the crazy one! Everyone's family is crazy, right? How often do we inevitably say, "Oh my god, my family is the weirdest!"? We don't get to choose our family members. We're stuck with them through thick and thin, for life. There's plenty of love/hate going around. Unless you come from a dysfunctional and potentially toxic background (like I did), most families are an incredible combination of fun, supportive, crazy, frustrating, annoying, and wonderfully special. There are so many aspects of your life that you carry with you forever that come from your special family members.

Your Relationship with Your Parents

The relationship with your parents is complex, complicated, and multi-faceted. This relationship literally covers your entire life. It's crazy to think of it in those terms, right? Your parents, assuming they fruitfully live well into their golden years, will literally be there for you for the vast majority of your life. Think about that. We take this for granted, unfortunately. This is truly a special relationship. Think about the fact that you have perpetual support of parents who are always there for you. But most of the time, you don't realize that or think of it in those terms. But it is truly special.

This is a relationship that truly has to be cherished and nurtured. You have to give thanks to your parents on a daily basis. They not only created your life, they nurtured you, raised you, guided you, and supported you in all ways (particularly financially). If that's not enough, they'll probably leave you a decent inheritance. Knowing all this, how can you not have anything but love, respect, and eternal gratitude for your parents? If you have anything less than that for them, then you truly need to look at yourself in the mirror and quickly address the problem that requires your immediate attention and resolution. They are your blood, you are theirs, and it's the same and shared blood of family. That alone deserves the ultimate respect and appreciation. Family is everything! No truer words have been created.

My only suggestion to you is, if you have any unresolved issues with your parents, big or small, please force yourself to face this truth and start addressing it. Take the initial and small step that is needed in order to set you on the path of resolution and reconciliation. You will forever have guilt and remorse if you don't accomplish this task before their passing. Save yourself the eternal guilt by taking care of this problem. No matter the issue or who's to blame, YOU are the one who needs to take the first step. Your parents deserve the small amount of respect for you being the one to start the process, even if they are factually 100% to blame. They've earned the right for their child to make the bold first move. After all, they need to be and you need them to be eternally in your life, particularly if you have children. Their grandchildren need the love and support of their grandparents, just like you had.

The Relationships with Your Siblings, Cousins, and Extended Family

Your siblings are a continuation of your crazy family. They are literally your brothers and sisters for life. They are your first friends of your life, and they will probably be your last friends too. The sibling bond is oh so special, if you allow it to be. Sibling rivalries can unfortunately ruin the relationship on a permanent basis. These rivalries are typically rooted in the jealousy and envy of the relationships with their parents that exist among the siblings. However, if you have the strong support of your parents, usually these rivalries can be overcome and buried.

The special feelings and level of support that you get from a big brother or a big sister are so inspiring and reassuring. Many times they can serve as your first exposure to learning how to become confident. Your big brother or big sister can inspire you (if not force you) to push yourself beyond your fears. They can also serve as corroboration of the things that your parents are trying to teach you, since your older siblings would have experienced those teachings before you. The sibling relationship will grow into adulthood in a way where you continue to be each other's cheerleader. Many times, your sibling also becomes a second parent or an extension of your parent, especially when a parent passes. You always have each other to commiserate and share the thoughts and feelings that you may not want to discuss with your parents. Similarly, you can commiserate about your parents as well. As it is said, the sibling relationship is from cradle to grave.

Sometimes if there's a large age gap between siblings (like in my case, being the far youngest of three), the relationship may not be as strong of a bond as one where they are closer in age, but it is still a very special one in other ways. The large gap relationship can serve as a quasi-parent relationship. There is nothing wrong with an additional quasi-parent who is there to love and support you. Any and every type of sibling relationship is crucial in your growth and development. You can learn so many additional aspects of life that you may or may not attain directly from your parents. You'll also learn from the successes and failures of your siblings as well. The more members there are in your immediate family, the more learning and growth is inherent in this environment. Cherish those sibling relationships.

When it comes to your cousins, they are like your additional brothers and sisters, but on a part-time basis. You don't necessarily live and/or grow up with them, but you get to share your lives with them in similar ways as your siblings, but typically without any sort of sibling-type rivalries. Your cousins can become your first confidant-type friend. You'll share things with your cousin that you wouldn't with anyone in your immediate family. You'll have different and unique experiences with them that you wouldn't with your siblings.

Before you establish your first friends outside of your family, the cousin relationship will be the first time that you'll see how other families are raised different than your own. You'll begin to realize that every family is different and that the dynamics of every family environment can be vastly different than your own. This will be your first exposure to hopefully feeling grateful about your own family dynamic once you witness one that you feel is different in ways you don't agree. You'll begin to appreciate your life and your family. Or the opposite may true, you'll start to realize that there are elements of your family dynamic that could be improved.

The parents of your cousins, who are your aunts and uncles, are another set of relationships in your life. Your aunts and uncles can be another set of amazing adults who provide you with love and support. They can be your part-time parents. In some cases, they feel like your permanent parents because you spend more time with them than you do with your parents, who may be working prolonged periods (like in my case growing up; my aunt always felt like my second mom, sometimes my first). If you are fortunate enough to grow up in a family that also includes a large extended family with cousins, aunts and uncles, you are in an amazing position to have so many people in your life who love and support you. It's important to take advantage and cherish every single one of those relationships because they will forever help you in the long-term. You'll always have someone you can turn to. You'll have an incredibly vast support system of parents, siblings, cousins, and aunts/uncles.

I am fortunate that my children are growing up in such an extended family. They have both their parents, each other, their grand-parents, many cousins, and many aunts and uncles. It is truly a special and amazing dynamic. Every family get-together is one where they all feel the love and support of each other. Your children are always better served when they grow up with as many people around them who unconditionally love and support them. Everyone benefits from such an extended family environment. As adults, they will continue to have many loving family members that they can turn to for consistent support and guidance on a daily basis. It is truly a remarkable dynamic. While family is everything, the more members in that family the better for everyone. The bigger the better…

"…Love immeasurably."

TIBETAN PROVERB

"Being deeply loved by someone gives you strength,
while loving someone deeply gives you courage."

LAO-TZU

STAGE 9:

The False Identity Crisis (The Career Identity Fallacy)

What does your government issued identification card say about you? Absolutely nothing, there's no identity there of you. So what is your identity then? Do you identify yourself with having one? Can you define it? For most, it's difficult to define who you are.

Your authentic self and the identity with which you are aligned should be one in the same. A person's true and real identity is many times not in line with the actual life that a person is living. Whether or not you are aware of a disconnection determines the next course in your life. If you are aware and believe you're not living your true life, that awareness is the beginning of making the choice to change your course. If you're not aware, then hopefully this section will force you to ask deep-level questions of yourself for you to realize that you may be living under a false identity crisis.

The false identity crisis is when a person is living a life and an identity that is contrary to the inner, authentic identity of that person.

Many times, this false identity crisis is directly linked with the career identity fallacy. A person's real identity should not be a function of his/her profession, career, or any type of influence of financial status, class status, position, power, or any other externally-derived association. An authentic and real identity should be and can be easily evident and exhibited by a person when he or she can freely talk about himself/herself without invoking any of these externally branded associations. When you can describe and define who you are without having to say what you do for a living, then that's when you know you're living your genuine life.

In any social setting where you're meeting new people, it is very common and normal for people to introduce themselves by saying what they do for a living. Very often when you meet a new person, inevitably the typical first question they'll ask of you is, "And what do you do?" This has always been one of my biggest peeves of every social setting. Why does your job/career have to be the most important aspect of who you are or the first way you define yourself to someone? In my first career as a corporate banker, I would routinely have to attend mixers. At these mixers, your career and position are always the crutch go-to questions. The vast majority of these people loved to talk about themselves — more specifically, they loved to talk about what they do, their jobs, and their careers.

I began to observe and realize that so many people defined themselves by simply what they do. Their identity *was* their career and vice-versa. That was it; that was literally the only way they identified themselves. It seemed so superficial to me. There didn't seem to be other aspects of who they were, other sides to their identity. During these conversations, I purposely would never say what I did for a living. I would deflect the question and start asking them other semi-personal questions, outside of their career, to get a better understanding of who they really were. After a few moments of discomfort on their part, they would inevitably come back to their job. I would acquiesce and put them out of their misery by engaging them in their "career" discussions.

While obviously what you do for a living is a huge part of who you are, as it should be, it's still never your entire identity, right? It can't be. Even if your career is your passion and you feel that you are exactly where you need to be, there are additional authentic versions of yourself beyond your career. For example, a professional athlete is one of the most difficult careers to achieve. Almost every professional athlete can say that they have achieved their ultimate goal since they were a child. They are making a living with their ultimate passion in life. It is tremendously difficult to get to a professional level of any sport, almost impossible. Less than one percent of the most elite and talented athletes make it to the professional level of any worldwide sport. The twelfth guy on an NBA bench who never plays and whose name you'll never know is still in that exemplary group of the less-than-one-percent category. It is an incredible achievement of which only an extreme select few can speak. Even in this prized instance, that still has to be just one side of that person's identity.

We are multi-faceted individuals. There are so many sides to the human life and to the human being. Unfortunately, many career-driven people, men and women alike, only see their identities through the eyes of their profession. They are so laser focused in their profession, that they forget some of their earlier passions in life when they were much younger. What's more is that in most of these situations, their laser focus comes to the detriment of spending less time with their spouses, families, and children. They're proud and boastful of their position and can only convey themselves to others through their status and position. They are somewhat disconnected from their families. When they finally retire, they feel lost. They feel like they've been stripped of their identity. That's because they have been stripped as far as they're concerned. They've only known that one side of themselves and never explored the other facets of their existence. They've only displayed that one side of themselves to others as well. They never paused in their life to ask themselves some of the deep-rooted questions of who and why they are.

They don't enjoy their retirement as they should by exploring and finding themselves. It's too late at that point. They don't have the drive and fortitude to switch gears and become a different person in their eyes. Sadly, even with family surrounding them, they don't feel like they have a purpose in life anymore. Without a purpose, a person will easily lose their will to live. Even with loved-ones surrounding them, they feel like they don't have a reason to live, so they don't anymore. They perish too soon with many years left to live.

This is the career identity fallacy. When you completely wrap yourself in only your career, you've created a fallacy in your life that makes you believe you're not allowed to be anything more than how you see yourself in your career. I left a twenty-year corporate career that I loved because I felt like it was stifling me in my pursuits and interest of other passions. Although I had felt that way for many years leading up to it, you still have to muster a great deal of strength, belief, and conviction to leave a comfortable career that is providing well for your family and children. It takes an incredible amount of belief in yourself, your vision, and the support of your significant partner and family members. Fortunately, I had and still have that in my life and was able to use their support and my belief to pursue additional passions of mine.

Our careers should not define us. What we believe and what we stand for should be the start of what defines us. We are so much more than what earns us an honest pay to provide for ourselves. Your identity is an ongoing process. It's never finite or linear. Working on it means constantly refining it and re-defining it. It is a dynamic, organic, and ongoing process.

Asking yourself how you would want to engage life is a good starting point. It is also a good question to keep asking yourself throughout the process. There are five intrinsic ways to proceed with the ongoing life-long process of defining who you are: (1) reflecting, (2) deciding what you want, (3) making (better) choices, (4) pursuing/exploring your passions, and (5) developing your social circle. At the end of this process, there's a simple answer to the question of who you are. That answer is "I am me." The key is to know your "me" at that point.

Reflecting means you have to look at the person in the mirror facing you. You have to ask that person hard-hitting and revealing questions. You have to be brutally truthful with your answers. You have to strip away all your self-denials. You have to be honest about your strengths and your weaknesses. Being honest about your weaknesses is the hardest part. You have to define in which areas of your life you are unhappy. You don't have to address them just yet. This is the stage of reflecting and the revelations you realize about yourself.

Deciding what you want and who you want to be is the next phase. Perfection is impossible and being a perfect person is not achievable. However, you can create and pursue a strong and diligent work ethic that strives for perfection with the understanding that it is not completely achievable. Your efforts, work ethic, and follow-through can be and should be perfect. 100% effort is perfect; the process can be perfectly followed without a perfect end result. What type of engagement do you want in life and who is the person you want to be leading the way?

Start making better choices. Redefine what matters to you and accept that certain things will have to go. You cannot make the mistakes of the past. This new path requires better decision making and better choice making. Define and be clear of your values so your decisions will align with those values. When you know who and what you want to be, you can make the specific and direct choices that will place you on the path of the ultimate destination. For example, if what you want to be requires higher education of some type, then you have to be honest with yourself about going back to school. That decision will then form the additional related decisions in terms of the life you will now have while in pursuit of that person you want to be.

Exploring and pursuing your passions will help you find your right path. It will also help you realize that you may have many passions, some or most of which you'll want to pursue as well. If you don't know what your passions are from the outset, you need to start focusing on the areas of life that you really enjoy, the areas where you usually find yourself being lost and happy. These are the areas that make you feel good and consistently bring you joy, contentment, and peace of mind. This exploration will help you identify your passions. Developing a growth mindset is a key component of exploring your passions. A growth mindset is one in which you are constantly growing, maturing, and learning from your prior experiences, and particularly learning from your mistakes. It is important to always maintain a growth mindset, one in which challenges become opportunities for growth. This growth occurs beyond your comfort zone and thereby reinforces your discipline to this mindset, which further serves as motivation to stay disciplined. You alone are creating your world of experience, and you are in control of it.

The final phase of developing your social circle helps to create a support system that validates your choices and who you are. A support system is always vital in helping you stay on course when the process becomes more challenging. Your family is the best support system in most cases. However, in creating a strong social circle of friends beyond your family, it is important to (1) disassociate yourself from people who you believe might get in the way of your goals and (2) align yourself with like-minded people who share similar paths as you. You want to make sure that you have a social circle and support system of people who are pushing you forward and not holding you back.

The false identity crisis in which your career becomes your only hallmark and calling card will prevent you from living your true self. While usually it is someone's career that creates a fallacy of your identity, the false identity crisis can take other general forms in which you are not living the life of the person you wish to be. You might be wearing a mask or many masks, which can become a normal way of life for you. This is a very difficult, and ultimately, a debilitating way to live one's life. It may be difficult to come to this awareness initially when self-denial has been so deep-rooted in you. If there's even a bit of a sense where you feel that maybe your life isn't quite right and you're not sure why, you should start asking yourself honest questions. Don't be afraid to look in the mirror, literally face yourself, and look straight into your own eyes when asking questions of yourself.

This is when you'll start to see some of the truths that have been buried in years of self-denial. This will be the start of you scratching the surface of who you think you are. Do not be afraid to continue peeling the layers. It will scare you, but ultimately, it will give you the belief in yourself that you've needed. This belief and the follow-through of the process will free you. It will be liberating and life-changing. You'll end up asking yourself why you didn't start this process much sooner. You'll need to surround yourself with the inner circle and support system of deeply trusted people. Life's challenges become easier to tackle when you have the help and support of people who believe in your pursuit. Before you know it, your past false identity will be summarily destroyed while the birth of the pursuit of your authentic identity has begun.

"Knowing yourself is the beginning of all wisdom."

ARISTOTLE

STAGE 10:

Your Relationships with Money, Materialism, Addictions, and Social Media

What can I tell you in this Stage that you haven't heard already as you were growing up? Actually, quite a bit, some of which hopefully you're fully aware. I don't have to tell you that life is not about materialism, superficiality, and the pursuit of money. Even the most materialistic person might agree with the notion of that statement. But really living this notion is another matter entirely.

I can sum up this Stage by simply saying, "Stop focusing on objects and money, and start focusing on the real things and people who matter in your life." That is also mostly a superficial statement. We have to dig deeper and discuss the reasons why so many people gravitate towards and are attracted by the pursuit of money, power, and status. I have to admit, they are very alluring, enticing, and seductive; otherwise, they wouldn't be called temptations.

Life certainly can be and is to many people about nothing more than materialism. They live their entire lives as such and ultimately die in the same manner, thinking that they've left behind some sort of legacy. They die never realizing that the material legacy they've left behind will only last but for a short while, and this time frame is proportionally congruent to how much and how fast their heirs will blow through that legacy. There is no eternal, life-fulfilling legacy to speak of that is left behind unfortunately. Their names and memories are soon forgotten. A legacy of only money and no meaning or worth is not much of a legacy. I hope that my words will spark a thought process for these people before their time expires. This spark might become a fireball in their hearts and minds to perhaps form a new perspective on their wealth and materialism.

Don't get me wrong, there's nothing wrong with creating and having wealth and possessions, especially if that wealth and monetary success is a result of hard work and diligent commitment. In fact, I wish for every human on earth to be in a position of ultimate financial independence. While monetary wealth can become a fortunate by-product of a life well-lived, it should not be the driving force of life itself. True financial independence doesn't necessarily mean mega riches and significant wealth, although it can. It simply means being wise enough to manage your money, assets, and liabilities in such a way that you ultimately eliminate all your liabilities. This is financial independence, when your money and assets are freely unencumbered. There's nothing wrong in taking care of your money and financial position. We live in a currency-driven world. Taking care of your overall self should include your financial well-being as well.

Here is the simple, clear, and unequivocal difference in the perspective of being materialistic and attached to your money and possessions versus simply having material things in your life. The most genuine and authentic way of creating and arriving at monetary success comprised of financial independence and at least moderate wealth is through creating something of value that helps and serves people. In other words, this is the primary goal, to help and serve people in the most genuine and empathic way possible. When this is done the right way, success always naturally follows. When success happens, financial and monetary success comes with it as well. When you do something right and the right way, it is bound to be both successful financially and practically.

Creating value is the key, for yourself and for others. The best way I can describe the perspective you should have with money is as follows: view money as a meaningful creation and exchange of value, not dollars signs or the amount in your bank account. When you view money as value you create, share with others, or receive in return, that's when materialism exits the equation, along with your attachment to it.

As an entrepreneur for example, my number one priority was to always think about the customer. The business was a function of the customer being in the dead center where I established a long-term relationship with every single customer. My philosophy was simple. If I conduct business the right way and always do the right things in service of my clients (with no deviation), then the monetary success will automatically come with it. In other words, when done right, success is the given result. When done wrong, as in focusing on the maximum amount of money I can extract from a client, success may come, but is almost always short-lived. My goals, business plans, and projections were never about the money; it was always about the value and service I bring to my clients. When you have that as the focus, everything else naturally falls in line, including financial success. This approach all starts with my intrinsic passion of helping people, which is precisely why I've taken this passion to the next level by writing this book.

It's the same principle in team sports for example. When an unselfish player doesn't care about his personal statistics and success, and only focuses on the team's success as the primary goal, not only does the team succeed, but the statistics and accolades naturally bring success to that player as well. Magic Johnson (my sports hero) was the greatest example of this type of unselfish leadership. He was the epitome of consistently focusing on making every single teammate around him better. He knew that if he made his teammates better, the team will succeed, and that his own success will naturally follow. He elevated and empowered people, in the same way that Abraham Lincoln did with his cabinet and country. LeBron James is the present-day version of such unselfish leaders.

When you do become financially successful through hard-earned, genuine means of helping people, you still have to be diligent in keeping with your core philosophy. What can typically happen with financial success, even for non-money motivated people, is being swayed by the allure and seduction of money, materialism, status, and power. People look up to you and hail you as a successful person. That type of success and adoration can fool you into thinking that you don't have to be the same person anymore that you were before the financial success. You start valuing money more, you start buying expensive and fancy objects, and you start amassing meaningless symbols of wealth. The worst part is you start believing that you are higher in status than other people and you stop treating them as equals. You've completely forgotten who you were from this materialistic transformation. You've become singularly attached to your money and possessions and have become detached from your meaningful connections with people.

The word "relationship" is a powerful word that holds the understanding to the bond and attachment of the two parties in the relationship. You have to look at your money in the form of a relationship with it. The question becomes, what kind of relationship do you want that to be? Do you want a co-dependent one where your attachment becomes a life-and-death struggle? Or do you want a healthy and independent one where you look at your money and possessions as nothing more than a fleeting means of accessibility? When you are co-dependent, your life literally revolves around the item to which you are dependent. When that item loses value, you become deflated, angry, and frustrated, and you lash out at your loved ones as an entitled tyrant. When it gains value, you fall into a false state of happiness and temporal joy. It's like a drug because that feeling of fake euphoria does not endure. If that item were to go away completely from your life, you might as well consider yourself entirely lost as well. It could be so devastating and deflating that you either resort to death-wish type behavior or you might consider doing the deed yourself.

As with any relationship in your life, you must have a strong mutual respect and understanding of each party in that relationship. You have to have enough self-respect and belief in yourself to look at your money as completely detached from you. In fact, you have to look at it beyond just this state of detachment. You have to look at your wealth and means as a source for not only yourself and your loved ones, but a possible source for others who can benefit from your generosity. When you have an understanding and respect for your money, you always feel free and liberated enough to entertain any thought of its use, beyond just your own. In fact, you start looking for ways where your resources can start benefiting others, and hopefully mankind on a larger scale. Once you create that sense of appreciation of your hard-earned resources, you realize that the way to hold onto to this relationship is *not* by wrapping your impenetrable arms firmly around it, but to leave it in the open, where it feels the warmth of fresh air instead of the musty feel of a locked vault.

Understanding and knowing that your money can easily disappear at any point, relieves you from the unnecessary burden of tightly holding on to it. Moreover, you know that even if and when it's gone, you have the ability, faith, and spirit to create more of it. You don't even skip a beat in this process. When you've integrated this awareness, you'll have a healthy, detached relationship with your money. With this type of relationship, you won't be living in fear of losing. Instead, you'll enjoy life's pleasures with it, and you'll be able to live in the moment of true appreciation. True appreciation is knowing that the moment can be and will be lost forever. But when you truly live and breathe in the moment, you will never lose the memories of it. The memories serve as the link to the next cherished moment. When you've finally savored your last memory before passing on and leaving your legacy behind, it will be a legacy filled to the brim with everlasting love and eternal appreciation of the person you were. Your name will be remembered, spoken of, and live on through generations.

Monetary wealth is not the goal in the life. Wealth of life is the goal. The more wealth of love, people, memories, meaning, and awareness with which you're able to surround yourself, the richer your life. Do you want to be rich in life or rich only in money? Bob Marley said it best. "Some people are so poor all they have is money." If all you have and all you value is money, you will still be poor in life. People say that money will buy you happiness. Or it can at least rent happiness for a while. But the truth is that your life is not about the quest of finding happiness just as much it's not about the quest of building monetary wealth. Happiness is not meant to be found; it is meant to be arrived at. When you arrive at happiness, it is ever-lasting and not ethereal. Happiness is a function of joy. Joy is fulfilling and lasting. Once you feel joy, you'll be automatically happy. The quest is to find joy. And that quest is made easy when you focus on unearthing and living your authentic self. When you're content with yourself knowing that there's no other way you would want to be, joy emanates from within you. You feel joyful and appreciative of your life. As such, you arrive at happiness because it's simply there waiting for you. You won't be able to hide your permanent smile from happiness; you'd be fooling yourself if you tried.

Addictions

Addictions can manifest in many ways. They are the poisons of life. Your financial status is not a determinate factor of or a precursor to additions. It's important to address the relationship you may or may not have with addictions of any type. Yes, relationship. Even if you're not an addict and never have been, it's important to know that there's still a relationship that exists, one that requires you to know that addictions can befall on anybody. Hopefully, that is the extent of your relationship. For those who are recovering addicts or you are struggling with addiction, it's important to expose, understand, and manage your addiction on a daily basis.

If you've never been an addict, bless you. You should be very proud of yourself. At a minimum, you need to understand the insidious power of addiction, what addicts go through, and that you need to continue to live in a way that avoids the gravitational pull of an addiction. While I can't speak as a recovering addict myself, I can speak as a survivor adjacent to one. I've been surrounded by addicts in my life, particularly my father and brother. Fortunately, I was able to decide at a young age that I didn't want to live my life like my alcoholic father. I made sure I took measures in my life to avoid the typical pitfalls of such an addiction. By fortune, perseverance, and a strong will, I grew into a healthy young adult without being influenced by the allure and pull of addiction. Because I created a specific template of addiction avoidance at a young age, I was able to permanently hard wire that template as a guide for my entire life.

It's easy for someone like me to just simply say to avoid the known pitfalls of addiction, but I know the reality of the situation is far from such a simple, banal statement. The problem for most people is that they are typically pulled by addiction at a young age when they haven't formed a defense and strategy against it. I was lucky. Some of us are. Many of us are not. If you've grown up in an environment of addiction, it becomes easier to fall victim to it. Addiction victimizes the user. Once you become a victim, it becomes very difficult to impossible to extract yourself from it without third-party support and intervention.

I learned long ago from a recovering addict that addiction has a basis in genetics, not in the sense that it's hereditary (although that can certainly also be the case), but by the fact that our predisposition to falling prey to addiction is in our genes. In other words, those who are genetically more easily predisposed to addiction have a higher risk of falling prey to it. Those who don't could still fall prey to it given the habit-forming escapism of addiction. The problem is we don't know and can never know what lies in our genes. At a minimum, we need to understand this relationship to have respect for the risks of addiction. This is not only for our sake but for the sake of knowing how to be helpful and supportive of our loved ones and friends of addiction.

Most of us know by now that addiction is classified as a disease, and rightfully so. It has been medically proven that the body is clinically and physiologically addicted to the substance and/or behavior in question. In other words, no matter how powerful your mind, there is no amount of strong will power that alone will extricate you from any addiction. Sadly, even though we know this to be true, people (including your loved ones) might still view your addiction as a shameful, controllable pattern of behavior, instead of an actual disease, like every other disease. When a person contracts a disease of any type, the first order of business is to get clinically diagnosed, and then prescribed with the medication that will start to cure and/or manage the disease. We have to view addiction in this manner.

We have to start the process of "medication" for our loved one with an addiction. The biggest difficulty and difference with this type of disease is that the "medication" needs to be first accepted and acknowledged by the addict to be the cure. In other words, the addict has to come to an awareness and acknowledgement (mostly of their own volition) that there is a medical issue that needs to be addressed with adequate third-party support and management. This is the most difficult and excruciating process for all parties concerned.

My biggest advice for all parties is to never lose hope. Continue in your persistence and insistence of helping and supporting the addict. There will be many failed attempts along the way, but hopefully most of those will serve as learning lessons and building blocks for the next more successful attempt. The relationship of addiction becomes one in which there are hopefully more people than just the addict and the disease. The relationship should be one of a strong support system that continues to forge through until getting to the other side of recovery. Once on the other side, take a very quick breath and continue your vigilant support because the recovery process can be long and difficult as well. As they say, you can only take it day by day at this point.

The reason why I included the topic of addictions in this Stage of your relationship with money and materialism is because a very common pattern that typically occurs is people falling into addiction once they've acquired material wealth. Their relationship with money is a co-dependent, materialistic one, and so therefore, they are more prone to be seduced by the materialism, accessibility, and escapism of addiction. It is vital to understand the all-encompassing relationship that comprises money, power, and status. It's important, but very difficult, to consistently maintain top of mind that a healthy relationship with your money is one in which you completely detach yourself from it, its power, and seduction. If you simply continue to live your authentic life on the same path, it will not be difficult to avoid the negative influences and seductions of affluence and unlimited access.

Your Relationship with Social Media

In simplest terms, your relationship with social media should be of not having one. In other words, while having a social media presence is perfectly fine, your relationship with it should be one where you don't think of it as a relationship that you must have in your life. While your real-life relationships with the important people in your life should be treasured and nurtured, the best way to nurture your social media relationship is to acknowledge and remember that it is not needed in your life and that you are not dependent on it. Your self-worth and validation come from within you and your inner circle of your most valued relationships. Social media need not play a part in that, not one iota.

Social media is simply a technological tool in your life, nothing more, in the same vain as all other technological tools utilized for enhanced communication. Your perspective and usage of social media should be essentially the same as your other communication devices/options such as a cell phone, tablet, computer, email, messaging, etc. When understanding and accepting this perspective, there are fundamentally three types of relationships you can have with social media: (1) business, (2) personal, or (3) both.

Social media is best utilized as a business relationship. Connecting with your customers/followers and promoting your brand parlay perfectly with the benefits that social media provides. By nature, when you maintain a business relationship of any kind, you keep your private life completely removed from your business endeavors. Because of this inherent and natural detachment, you never feel psychologically dependent on it nor obligated to it in any way. The constant state of objectivity lends itself to being a constructive tool that greatly benefits your business goals. Consequently, you never feel compelled to share your private life nor seek any type of internal validation via this external venue.

To that point, a personal relationship with social media is not necessary, because after all, what is it that you are seeking if all of your business needs are already met? Nevertheless, it is not that simple is it? Just like with many other aspects of our lives that are not necessary, we are easily inclined to partake in them, especially when everyone else has partaken. In today's digital and virtual age, many people have created a personal relationship with social media whereby they communicate virtually with friends and followers they have established online, on a regular basis. Sharing your private life has become the norm, a potentially risky and dangerous one. Where is the healthy boundary line of your private life online? Is there a healthy boundary line? It is a very challenging task indeed; and it is multi-layered with many ramifications, consequences, and dependencies.

The healthiest boundary line that ensures zero risk of any kind would be not to share any of your private life whatsoever. However, if you choose to share your private life, you have to be diligent and extremely prudent with this sharing to mitigate potentially negative consequences. It is a very delicate and difficult balancing act on a tightrope. If you are not completely confident in your self-worth, it can become an insidious task that envelopes you, leaving you a victim of its co-dependent trap.

Just like with any other aspect of your life in which one may become co-dependent and/or develop an addiction, your social media relationship can transition into a co-dependent and/or an addictive one. The most important and determinative question is: who is in complete control of your life? Are you in control or is social media controlling you? If you are living your life in a way where your immediate thought is to always share it online and/or check in on a frequent and unreasonable basis, then you are not in control. Social media should be an after-thought, not the primary thought. It should be an enhancement or an auxiliary to your life, not a dependent reliance on it. The private life that you choose to share should be one that conveys and exhibits it from an undeniable perspective of self-worth and self-confidence, not one that appears to be vying for attention and validation.

If your daily behavior exhibits addictive patterns, then you must be honest with yourself and acknowledge that *your relationship with social media* is an unhealthy one. Your physical and mental health is of utmost importance. Therefore, you need to be strong enough in that moment of realization to start taking corrective action and/or seek help to change your course. As difficult as it may be to change your course, you must remember that your virtual life can be turned off with a simple key stroke. Your focus should be back on your REAL life, surrounded by the real people of your inner circle. Once you shift your focus back to what is real and important in your immediate life, the virtual one will become distant and non-existent. Continue to lean on your family and support system. They will help you re-connect with your self-worth and confidence. Once that happens, you will remember and re-connect with the fact that your relationship with social media should be of not having one.

"Materialism coarsens and petrifies everything,
making everything vulgar, and every truth false."

HENRI FREDERIC AMIEL

STAGE 11:

Live from Love Not Fear (Destroy Your Survival-Based Default)

We all hold the tremendous power of love in us. We all hold the tremendous power of loving others. It comes so easily and naturally for us to love the people within our inner circle of family, significant partners, and close friends. Why is it then so excruciatingly difficult to treat a fellow human being with love as the default mode of approach and behavior? At a very minimum, why is it hard for us to give a person the benefit of the doubt from love, before we decide otherwise?

Many of mankind's ills, starting with ancient civilizations to modern day, can be attributed to the survival-based psyche of the human mind. Allow me to explain. Man's life-and-death survival in pre-historic time was the predominant and highest priority. Every day was literally a fight for survival to be able to live one more day. This innate survival instinct is a function of fear. Fear was the main motivation and everyday catalyst to consistently reside in survival mode.

Unfortunately, during the course of man's evolution from pre-historic to ancient civilizations to our modern civilization, this fear-based survival instinct continued to remain part of our psyche. It is still the primary thought process that we initially default to when encountering a new, unknown situation, before our minds are able to pause and re-analyze the situation to realize that there is no fear or threat posed. In other words, our default and instinctual fear-based survival kicks in and we consequently make wrong and uninformed decisions, many of which prove to be devastating and annihilating against other people. Fear-based decision making never allowed for goodness and prosperity to have a fighting chance of becoming the way of civilizations; instead, the conquering and dominance of others became the norm.

For example, since the beginning of time, whenever a human came across another human in a new region, who was not part of his "clan" and who looked and acted different than what he knew to that point, the initial instinct was to fear the other person. Thus, that first meeting is adversarial instead of communal. The two humans approach each other with guards up instead of arms open. An enemy is created instead of a friend. Fear and survival override love, curiosity, and the desire to understand their differences. These differences stir up fear, shock, and the protection of oneself instead of invoking and seeing the natural awe and beauty of our diversity. Wars ensue, the need to conquer the other becomes the norm as civilizations are raided and devastated. Empires are built from such conquering, thus never allowing people from unrelated regions to meld together in harmonious acceptance of their differences.

Even when empires fell and the democratic countries of today's modern age became the norm, the deep-rooted and fear-based psyche that people still harbored continued to prevent neighboring countries to act as harmonious neighbors. Hatred, bigotry, and racism still continued to persist and drive the prevailing narrative. The fear of someone not like yourself still served as the primary motivator to rationalize the non-acceptance of people not like yourself. Added to this equation was the great significance of different religions, the combination of which fueled an evil-based rationalization of the slaughter of other people, who were no less innocent than the conquerors before their genocidal acts.

Religious-based wars corroborated the general war mentality of "solving" differences, instead of allowing for alternate paths of peaceful resolution. Once the concept of war was rationalized as a normalized method of dealing with other peoples, the simple and basic premise of accepting other people as the first option (before the start of any self-imposed discord and conflict) became completely obsolete and non-existent in the minds of people and their leaders. Once normalized and perpetuated, newly-born generations who were never the instigators of such wars, nor who understood the reasoning behind them, nevertheless continued (in their herded sheep-like mentality) their ancestors' ways of righteous indignation and rationalization of continued acts of atrocities against innocent people.

In short, that was a long-winded way to simply say that we should be living our lives love-centered, not fear-based. We should be guided by our hearts of understanding, not our fears that shroud us in armor. The word "heart" after all, has "art" in it, and art is truth at its core. Being guided by truth makes it easier and simpler to live a life when living it from a love-based center. Love is true, it is genuine, and it can be unconditional, which is a rarity because most things in life are not unconditional. Love taps into your empathy and brings it to the forefront of your behavior with people. When you have an open heart, you inherently care for others. If you really think about it, is there any negative aspect of love itself that you can think of? No, not at all. The only downside to love is that someone can misuse it against you, but even then it has nothing to do with you. You're not the abuser of love in this case.

The overall general sense of love that we possess should be our default instinctual behavior towards others, just as it is for our family members and close friends. This type of love, care, and concern should be an extension towards all humanity, no matter the race, ethnicity, religion, gender, sexual affiliation, etc. Clearly, I'm not talking about romantic love that you have for a partner. That kind of love is a function of an emotion that is born, nurtured, and fostered toward a specific individual with whom you want to share such a love. The love I'm describing that we should all inherently bear is a state of being, nothing more and nothing less. In fact, we all have it. We just need not be afraid to live with it as our center of being towards others.

We are all born with love, every single one of us almost 8 billion people on Earth, whether we admit it or not. The moment a newborn looks into the eyes of their parents, that look is 100% pure love. A baby literally knows nothing else in that moment. They are born with love and they bond to us with their love. If we are born with it, why do we lose it for people outside of our family and close friends? How can we be so arrogant, so uncaring, so entitled, and so inhuman to "believe" that our fellow mankind doesn't deserve our same love? I placed "believe" in quotes because that's exactly what unfortunately happens. From birth, our every single point of reference that we have with people and the outside world unfortunately brainwashes us into the false narrative that anyone other than in your immediate trusted circle does NOT deserve our same love in anyway, or at least the benefit of the doubt of having our love. We are instead taught to tread carefully, to be guarded and make sure we alleviate our fear of the unknown person before we give them any benefit of the doubt whatsoever.

That is the problem and that is the crux of it. Not only are we taught this inane fallacy, but we're further brainwashed to believe that the other person needs to "earn" our respect and love before we can hand it over. Does your newborn baby love you unconditionally from the very first moment setting eyes on you, or does that baby wait until it believes you have earned his love? Likewise, do you wait for your baby to earn your love? This ridiculous notion of respect needing to be earned is not only wrong but its origin comes from a skewed place. Our fear-based default and survival instincts have erroneously taught us that the person on the other side has to "earn" our respect first before we can proceed. How ridiculous is that? How about we change that narrative to what it should have been? We should approach every person with love, respect, and our open hearts. We should greet a person with: "Welcome to my world. I'm so happy to meet a fellow human being with whom I can learn and share our life experiences." Why can't the simplicity of common ground, shared experiences, and genuine communication serve as the default human interaction? Imagine a world where common ground is the point of genesis of human interaction between people unknown to each other.

I realize that there are bad seeds among us and that giving such a person the benefit of the doubt might and probably will hurt us in some way. Kindness should not be taken as weakness and/or naivety. However, that's an unfortunate part of humanity when the bad seeds take advantage of the good ones, which shouldn't discourage us from our path of openness and acceptance. Not everything is perfect. The minute someone disrespects us and/or takes advantage of us, we remove that person from our lives and simply move on. There's no need to engage in a war-like mentality. In fact, letting go of the anger should be the first step. We should also forgive that person for not knowing any better and have hope for his redemption, so that we don't carry any anger with us. For the really bad offenders and criminals, we have prisons. That type of person is the extreme minority of people. Why not welcome the unknown into our lives with open arms first? We have a justice system where one is presumed innocent, right? Why can't that principle be applied to everyday human interaction? Giving people the chance they deserve should be normalized.

Living with fear hurts us in many other ways. Fear stops us. Fear makes us cautious, distrusting, and ultimately hateful in many cases, sadly and unfortunately. It therefore complicates our lives unnecessarily and makes life more difficult to live. When love would have made for an easy, free, and simple life, now we've complicated everything in our life by allowing fear to dictate our interactions with people and all matters. Walls come up, borders are fortified, hatred is fostered, hatred becomes normalized, and preparedness for war as a flawed solution all set the stage for the next interaction, one born of hostility and enemy-making. The opportunity to become friends with our next-door neighbors never has a chance. It is never even a forethought of any kind.

If there are aliens in other worlds, I have a feeling they don't live their lives like humans do. That's why they've yet to engage us, if ever. They know that our immediate reaction to them will be contentious, adversarial, and one of wanting to destroy them. They are probably the opposite of us in their approach. If they were the same as humans, aliens would have engaged us thousands of years ago and most likely would have been the first to annihilate us. There are probably different types of aliens from different planets who have naturally accepted each other. They live harmoniously under the same universe because they love and respect their differences instead of being afraid of them. They realize the simple fact of resource sharing and collaboration to make for a stronger, better universe. This of course is an extreme metaphorical comparison of the way our humanity is versus how it could be.

Despite the nature of our human existence, we still individually have the power to change our discourse, our daily interaction with one another. We have the ability to re-program our default of fear (with crossed arms) to a core of love (with open arms and open heart). I would just simply say, why not try? What do we have to lose? We've lost so much already over thousands of years of our human existence, resulting in human suffering. Let's try to love each other. Let's eliminate the word "hate" from our collective dictionary. Just the elimination of that one word will deflate almost everything negative we've ever known. After all, don't forget the acronym of FEAR itself — it stands for "false evidence appearing real". Let that be your guiding truth.

*"The only thing we never **get** enough of is love;*
*and the only thing we never **give** enough of is love."*

HENRY MILLER

STAGE 12:

The Meanings of Life and Human Existence

Oh, the proverbial question, what is the meaning of life? Such a simple and short question, yet with so many answers.

The meaning of life is not absolute and singular. If it were, or if one wanted it to be, the simple answer is that the meaning of life is to always continue to search for the greater meanings. The proverbial quest "to find the meaning of life" is much more than just that simple phrase. There are many meanings of life and of human existence. For the human individual, there are several meanings in a person's life and one must strive to find and understand all their meanings, or at least as many as possible. Beyond the individual, there are also the greater meanings of mankind and human existence that one must strive to understand. The merged findings of both pave the path of your journey to greater awareness. This understanding assumes and includes a reconciliation of mankind's macro meanings vis-à-vis the individual's micro meanings.

Mankind's endless search for meaning since the beginning of time has certainly given us plenty of plausible understandings of life. But let's apply these understandings to the modern times of the lives we're living today. In the previous Stage, I described one of our most important greater meanings, which is to love and accept every human being unconditionally. But our past and current civilizations have equally proven that to be very difficult and impossible in many cases. However, our historical human failings shouldn't prevent you from accepting and applying this greater meaning in your life. If that were the only meaning you were to ever know, that wouldn't be so bad. You would certainly be a self-aware and self-actualized individual who clearly understands the greater good for mankind. You could basically stop reading at this point and live the rest of your life at peace, knowing that you're serving mankind well.

We need to dive and delve deeper in order to unearth a greater understanding of who you are, what your life is, and what that means for the rest of humanity. One of the meanings of life is simply the aforementioned: (1) who you are, (2) what your life is, and (3) what (1) and (2) mean for humanity.

Who you are is the theme of this entire book. It's difficult to understand any meaning in your life, let alone the greater meanings of life, if you don't know who you are. So who are you? If you're not able to answer that question, that's ok. It's not a finite process. It is an organic, ongoing process in which you continuously chisel away the clay to arrive at your masterpiece of a sculpture of you. The ideal process of unearthing who you are would start with your youngest age possible, meaning the moment you are able to think critically and analytically. The problem is most of us in our youth do not think in this way even though we possess the capacity. We aren't even aware we have this capacity. There is so much going on in the mind of a young person, that finding greater wisdom is not one of them.

It's unfortunate that wisdom and greater meanings come to us in our older age as we mature. Maybe it's because we start to sense our mortality, an awareness that doesn't exist in our youth. We think in terms of invincibility when we're young, instead of in terms of the fragility of life. Life is actually better learned in reverse, right? Our senior elders are wiser and have more to say about life than we could ever imagine. Why don't we learn from them, especially when they're constantly nudging us and trying to educate us? We don't have the time for them. That's what we feel. We feel like we're wasting time by hanging around old people. The worst part is young people don't even have the awareness that they will eventually become these same frail, older people one day, a day that will come much faster than they realize. The young ones are trying to seize the day and live their lives *their* way. Ancient cultures valued and the eastern cultures of today greatly value the elderly and their wisdom. They seek them out and seek for the wisdom being imparted onto them. Western cultures do not share that same reverence, appreciation, and desire of greater knowledge from our elders. That's clearly unfortunate.

This brings me to another meaning of life and a way of living that I believe to be significant in your growth and development. I learned this at a young age and incorporated it in my life immediately. Ever since my toddler years, I've always had an eagerness to learn by observation, meaning I literally watched other people and learned from them without having to first experience it myself. One of the first things I can remember teaching myself in this way was to learn how to play the drums. Every time I would listen to music and/ or watch a performance of musicians, I would myopically laser in on the sounds and physical movements of the drummer. I would mimic those movements to create the same sounds. Over time, I learned how to play the drums by ear. That first time of vigilant observance resulting in learned behavior motivated me to continue to use this observational way of learning.

As I grew into more of a critical thinker as a teenager, I adopted the following philosophy in my life: to learn from others before ever committing my own mistakes of trial and error in the first place. My tenet became the following in that there are three types of people in this world. The first is the one who makes a mistake, doesn't learn from it, and lives the rest of his life repeating the same or similar mistakes. This person is not the most intelligent, clearly. The second person is the one who makes a mistake, learns from it, and vows to never make it again. This person represents most of our population, hopefully. The third type is the one who learns from other peoples' mistakes first and vows to never commit them in the first place. This third person is how I patterned my life. Once you learn from others, why would you not avoid the learned mistakes of others and save yourself the time and aggravation in the first place? This is the more emotionally intelligent person with high intelligence, knowledge, and awareness. I've strived to be this person in my life as much as possible.

I've had the good fortune in my first career to adapt this principle on a daily basis. As a corporate banker, I spent countless hours with all types of companies and helped them improve their operational and financial positions. I was thus able to see the many managerial and financial mistakes that they had committed in the running of their companies. When I became an entrepreneur and ran my own businesses, I naturally avoided making these mistakes, thus saving my company time, money, and frustration. I was more successful because of this principle.

Learning from your own mistakes AND the mistakes of others along with the daily education from your keen observation is a meaning of life in and of itself. This meaning of life helps you grow and develop to continue to find additional meanings in your life and the greater ones beyond your life. Again, the earlier this meaning is adapted in your life, the better you are for it in your evolution.

Regardless of your age, it's important to integrate this principle in your life as soon as possible to place you on the path of self-awareness and self-actualization. While I would love for all young people in their 20's to start thinking about their lives on a greater level, to seek wisdom, and to seek the knowledge from their elders, I realize that it is not quite the easiest accomplishment. This reality and my awareness of it served as one of my primary inspirations to write this book. I'm hopeful that young readers of today's digital age will take to this book and try to incorporate what they learn from it early in their lives.

In your growth and development, as you're questioning who you are, you are chiseling away at that clay. Once you start following the path that you believe is more in line with your true and authentic life, you can start focusing on your life itself. You've either made a drastic change in your life once you figured out who you are, or you made a slight course adjustment that validated the fact you had started on the right path. You're now more aware of the actual life you're living. You start assessing and making sure your life includes every single loved one that you feel needs to be there. This can include your life partner, your children, your extended family, and your close inner circle of friends. When you feel totally complete and comfortable with your inner circle and support system, that is when you know you are living your true life and with the people that you want in it.

This doesn't mean that your life *has* to include other people who are loved ones. If you're a single person without an immediate family, you still have the family that created you and/or your extended family. You also have a tight circle of trusted friends perhaps. Even if you don't have any of that as a lone wolf, that is completely fine as well. Being alone is not at all a legitimate concern of any kind. It is not the same as being lonely. The most important relationship that you can have and should have is the unbreakable bond that you have with yourself first. You have to completely love yourself and respect who you are unconditionally and without question. Your value, worth, and meaning should be completely unquestioned in your mind. You have the strength, immense confidence, and conviction of knowing exactly who you are and what your life is. That is tremendous power, and you hold all of it. No one can take that away from you. It is infinitely yours. When you have that, you are never alone or lonely.

Depending on where you are in your life, the meanings of your life will differ from the next person. If you have a life partner and children for example, your meanings will certainly include these people. Your meaning will be that your life is a direct extension of their lives. Their welfare, care, and development will also be of paramount importance to you, just as much, if not more than your life. As a parent with children, you have witnessed the creation of and the miracle of life. Consequently, you have grasped this meaning as a fundamental basis in your life, which further helps you expand your meanings with your loved ones within the forever intertwined lives you will share together. If you don't have loved ones, then your meaning might be that your direction in life includes this goal at some point, and that the awareness of it is a vital meaning in your life. Or it might mean that you are completely contented in not having a life partner and/or children. Your complete conviction of that understanding is an important meaning in your life as well for you.

As a married person with three children, I certainly have become aware of the meanings in my life over time. They all have their origin and genesis from my marriage and the creations of life of my children. My first life before marriage created a new married life, which in turn, created another life of children and with children. The older we get and the more loved ones with whom we surround ourselves, the many more meanings become apparent and come to the forefront. As long as we are not living selfishly, we will easily see these meanings and happily accept them as our new meanings of life. Having an awareness of understanding and acceptance of the meanings of your life prior to the addition and inclusion of loved ones is vital.

Often times, people talk about their fear of commitment, which generally speaking, can be a fear of committing to anything, such as a person, a career, an accidentally unearthed identity of yourself, and/or anything else that may pose a fear for them. What they really mean is that they haven't yet understood the true meanings of their life in full, at this point in their lives. When you begin to see and understand these meanings in your life, commitment is no longer an issue. The fear disintegrates and disappears. Because once you find real meaning in your life, you actually long for commitment as you are ready for it. You seek it and you want it because you know you will thrive in a commitment, as it creates new meanings in your life. Finding meaning spurs the soul to continue to find more meanings, which requires commitments on your part. It becomes a reciprocating cycle and process, which forms into the organic process of growth and development.

What are the greater meanings for humanity and the overall human existence? For me, it starts with the small details, the very details of life and daily living. I've always been detail-oriented. It is the Type A personality in me. But I realized along the way of insanely being detailed that my focus on the finer details helped me to realize that life *is* actually about the finer details. When you think of the fact that there are almost eight billion people on earth, that thought alone is extremely overwhelming. You immediately feel like there's no possible way you can make a difference. But when you strip life to its core, to the details, particularly the details of your life, you find that it is not so overwhelming. You find that taking care of one detail at a time is all you need, akin to placing the pieces of the puzzle together one at a time. You have the awareness that the accumulation of all the little details result in a large masterpiece.

The details matter, your effort matters, your character in the moment matters. The way you act in any given moment when no one is looking is the way you act in every moment. Are your integrity and probity intact when no one is around? Or are you shedding the false veil of integrity and doing something you know is not right? All of these details and the many moments of your behavior all matter because they all add up to who you are and what you stand for. That pattern and result of who you are and what your life is form the way you treat and look at other people, and therefore how you view mankind on a greater level.

If you have genuine appreciation, respect, and hopefully love for your fellow human being, you will always treat everyone the same, no matter if eyes are on you or not. This approach also forms the legacy that you leave for your loved-ones because they will typically follow in your footsteps. Consequently, you are doing your small part in this world by allowing your life and your voice to be a great representation of how you treat people. With this value that you bring to people and to the world, you will have done your part for mankind. You will have served your purpose and lived a life full of many meanings, leaving a legacy for others.

Living a life that contributes to the service of others and to the world in some small way (or perhaps even a great way) is a fulfilled and actualized life that leaves behind a memorable legacy. When you can truly look at another human being as a fellow brother or sister and nothing more, you've achieved genuine understanding of who we are. When you don't see labels of any kind anymore, that's when your vision is a perfect 20/20. We are nothing more than humans. We are not labels, we are not male, female, republican, democrat, black, brown, white, Christian, Muslim, gay, transgender, young, old, etc. Even our given first names and surnames don't matter; they are also labels. They're completely irrelevant and random in their assignment. The absolute only reason for us to have given names is simply for there to be a word of reference to know who is being addressed. Our given names do not define us. Our fellow neighbors can be next door, the next state, in another country, or another part of the world unknown to us. It does not matter. The only thing that matters is literally the joy, happiness, and awe of seeing this neighbor, especially for the first time, and immediately becoming eternal friends with our neighbor. That's all that should matter. Imagine such a simple world. It need not be complicated by anything we falsely create; these are the complications that make our eyes see an enemy instead of a friend.

Ultimately, what are we talking about when we talk about all these meanings of your life and that of the greater life? It boils down to one simple premise. The goal is to arrive at wisdom and of the many meanings of life that come with it. Get there as soon as possible, but hopefully not right before death.

"Our prime purpose in this life is to help others.
And if you can't help them, at least don't hurt them."

THE DALAI LAMA

STAGE 13:

The Undeniable Belief in the Power of Miracles (The Reasons Why Things Happen to You)

What the heck is a miracle anyway? It means different things to people. I'll admit that this Stage is awkwardly titled, but I felt it needed to be titled exactly as I have it.

Remember my love for words? I felt like every word was needed in this title. I wanted to stress that (1) miracles have powerful effects and that there is a power in them, (2) an undeniable belief in their existence and their power is necessary to witness and experience them in your life, and (3) most of the reasons why things happen to you are because of miracles. Miracles are amazing. They happen constantly. Seeing them, embracing them, and understanding them will re-enforce the decisions you make in your life and the way you live your life. They are incredible reminders and validations that literally everything that happens to you has a reason behind it, good or bad. When you form an undeniable belief in the power of miracles and accept that they affect your daily life, you will begin to easily see them and seek them out.

Your life can be and will be forever changed when you allow miracles to come into your life. What is a miracle exactly? A miracle is any instance of an occurrence that can be viewed as a sign or message that represents, informs, and/or validates something else. These miracles can literally come in any form and shape as signs and messages, such as the following:

1.   Thoughts expressed by others and/or yourself.

2.   Something someone says on TV, online, video, radio, etc.

3.   An epiphany that you have out of nowhere.

4.   Something that stands out from a dream.

5.   Something happening on the road while driving.

6.   A situation that resolves on its own to your surprise and without your input. (This is my favorite miracle.)

7.   A surprise gift of money or otherwise.

8.   An occurrence you thought was bad only to realize it was good all along or turned into good.

9.   Being suddenly aware of the moment you're in and feeling a sense of joy or happiness as it is happening.

10. A memory being re-awakened.

11. Any reference or memory of a passed loved one.

12. An unexpected emotion that came on suddenly without warning.

13. Deja-vu.

14. A confirmation or validation of some type of you being correct on a matter.

15. Many, many other unexpected instances that surprise you.

The representation of their meanings can come from a basis of spiritual, religious, cosmic, practical, universal, energetic, or any other basis you choose to ascribe. It depends on your perspective and how you personally view the miracle. That's the beauty of a miracle. There need not be an exact explanation, because that is not the purpose of a miracle. The purpose is to understand the reason behind it, which is typically an affirmation or validation of some type. It validates a decision you have made to which you can tie this miracle. It supports your decision-making process, letting you know you're on the right track. It helps you to stay on track when you feel a sense of corroboration and relief by an external cosmic force.

I've personally been witnessing miracles throughout my entire life going as far back as I can remember. I began to notice miracles at a young age and I started to rely on them. Growing up in a tough environment, I longed for them to give me guidance. Every time there was tragedy or trauma, inevitably there would be some small moment of a miracle that would remind me that things will get better. I remember my lowest point in my life that came when I was a teenager. I got very despondent and depressed. I started to lose hope and thought of ending everything. I actually got very close to doing it when I suddenly remembered that I'll probably witness a miracle soon; I was relying on a sign to throw me off my course of misery. In that moment, it was only the hope of a miracle itself that got me through it, which was just enough for me to gather myself. That glimmer of hope was just enough.

The next morning, the miracle was self-evident. Upon waking, I immediately had a completely different perspective on life. I woke not feeling despondent anymore. I woke with a realization that my mother was greatly depending on me at that time, as she was suffering from significant mental illness (which ironically was one of the main reasons I was so depressed in the first place). I gained a greater awareness and understanding that my life was better served to help my mother. We gave each other life in that moment. That awakening was the miracle.

The greatest power a miracle holds is letting you know that everything will be ok. And most times, that's exactly what we need, nothing more. I can honestly say that almost in every instance in my life when I've been overwhelmed or have come to an impossible decision point, there was always a miracle of sorts to nudge me in the right direction or validate that I was doing the right thing. Many times it would actually resolve my dilemma unexpectedly for me. I gained a keen sense of awareness that I could rely on them, but never to do so in an objective, obvious, or an entitled way. I would rely on them without thinking about them. I tried to stay surprised and unaware by them. I began to view them as blessings for which I had to have great appreciation and gratefulness.

They occurred so often in my life that when I met and started dating my future wife at the time, I shared my miracle belief with her and told her she would start seeing them as well. I even jokingly referred to myself as the Miracle Man and started signing every greeting card as Your Miracle Man. When I knew I was going to marry her, I remember clearly telling her that she'll never have to worry about our life together because there would be many miracles to help us along the way. Every time one would occur, I would point it out to her as proof. She became a believer very quickly herself. To this day, I still point them out to her and/or remind her that things will be ok. Just watch out for another miracle as proof. They have become our blessings in our lives. To this day, I still sign all our birthday/anniversary/holiday cards as Your Miracle Man, and she refers to me in the same way.

There are reasons for every single thing that happens to you in life. I firmly believe that miracles are proof of that. Even though it's cliché to say "that happened to you for a reason," it is a true statement indeed. I've become so adept at spotting these reasons, that I do so almost immediately right after something good or bad happens to me or one my family members. If I can't see the reason in the moment, it typically reveals itself soon enough within a day or so. Looking for and being aware of a reason helps you to more easily accept a negative occurrence. Once you understand why something has happened, it's usually easier to accept it and to manage the acceptance process, no matter how bad. When you see additional affirmations and validations of those reasons by way of miracles and signs, you feel better about the reasons also.

You feel good from the validation that even though you experienced something negative, the reason provides proof that your life was meant to tread this course. It also validates that you are currently on the right path. Miracles occur so often in my life that I even see them occurring in reference to ordinary, daily, and mundane aspects of my life that don't carry much meaning. The more aware I've become of them, the more I actually see them in so many details of my life. It is truly amazing.

If you garner an undeniable belief in miracles, you will bear witness to their occurrence, to their powerful effect, and to their amazing explanations and validations of your own life to you. It is the equivalent of being able to look in a mirror and seeing your own life being reflected back at you, but with more clarity and vivid colors. In my case, I also have a religious and spiritual faith that serves as a basis for my belief in miracles. However, let me highly stress that you do not have to be religious nor spiritual in any way to witness the existence and power of miracles. Miracles do not discriminate; they manifest for believers and unbelievers alike. They are equal opportunity blessings for everyone. Please open your eyes to them. Start analyzing why certain things happen to you. Look for and dig deep to find the reasons behind every occurrence in your life. When you do, you'll typically find a miracle that is *not* trying to hide from you.

Miracles have a way of being there when you most need them, especially when you're on a new or unknown journey, or if you made a significant life change for example. They like to rear their heads and pop out when it's a new adventure for them. They get excited for something new. This is when they know that the person taking that adventure needs the most help, guidance, and assurance. The next time you venture out on a new road, such as the quest of unearthing your true self, don't be surprised to see miracles along the way. They will serve as your bumper guards to prevent you from slipping off the path. Every time you feel less hope or begin to doubt yourself, miracles will inevitably remind you of the awesomeness of your journey and to stay the course. All it takes is for you to witness and accept your very first miracle when it happens. The ones that follow will be self-evident and uniquely yours.

"Miracles happen every day, change your perception of what a miracle is and you'll see them all around you."

JON BON JOVI

"…in order to be a realist you must believe in miracles."

DAVID BEN-GURION

STAGE 14:

Men and Women are More Alike than They are Different

Who knows when the age-old gender debate between men and women started, but for it to ever have been a debate on a serious level, really? This Stage will be highly debated no doubt, as men and women since the beginning of time, have disagreed on many fronts, unfortunately.

At the core, men and women are both humans from the homo sapiens species, the last time I checked with science. The word "homo" literally means same. Humans are much more alike than we tend to acknowledge at times. Are we not the same? Since humans are alike, then men and women should be mostly alike. Logically that follows, but we must take a deeper dive on what I mean.

For the most part, men and women are much more alike than they are different. Let me repeat that. I'm not saying that we are alike, I'm saying that we are more alike than we are different. We are much more the same than we like to acknowledge. This is true for the simple reason that all of our basic needs as emotional and social human beings are essentially the same. We all need love, security, social connection, hope, purpose, respect, acknowledgement, praise, and not to mention the very basic needs of sustaining life. How are we different in any of these endeavors? We are not.

Men are typically wired not to display, share, and/or discuss some of these things. They tend to go about their daily life without much discussion of it. Their warped sense of masculinity makes them pre-programmed not to show much emotion, interest, curiosity, and most types of psychologically and emotionally-based points of discussion or exhibition. They have somehow been brainwashed during the evolution of humans that discussing and sharing anything beyond the objective, practical matters of life, particularly with the opposite sex, is a display of weakness and vulnerability. Men mostly do not share much with other men as well. No man wants to be the first to show any chink in his armor. At the core, men are sensitive and vulnerable, no less or no more than women, for the most part. Both men and women have sensitivity, vulnerability and empathy. If we are human, and we are, it is a given that both sexes are rooted in these basic feelings. Again, men simply choose not to display them as easily as a woman is able.

In their own privacy, when no one is around, men cry, they bawl, they feel vulnerable and victim to the many pains and wrongs bestowed onto them. I know this because I've done all those things and I know of other men who have also. When I open up to men and share with them some of my most sensitive moments, they inevitably start sharing as well. The walls easily come down. Now granted, some of us are more sensitive than others, but that's also true for women. There are different types of emotionally-based men as is the same for women. There are men who are more in tune with their "feminine" aspects, as there are women who display more "masculine" aspects of themselves, even though that's a horrible way to describe it. The words feminine and masculine shouldn't be used in those ways anyway; it's too stereotypical and offensive.

Physiologically and scientifically speaking however, men and women both have testosterone and estrogen. While one sex has more of one than the other, and vice-versa, this fact alone shows that men and women are mostly the same. Even though biologically we have different reproductive organs, psychologically, we share most of the same emotions and feelings because we both have the same hormones. While one hormone may be considered more male and the other is considered more female, nevertheless, we both have each.

We can even go back further, to the fetus stage of our lives. In this stage, the initial fetus starts out as one gender, and that gender is a female. Yes, we start out as females, not males. So doesn't it bear to reason that males are more similar to women than we would admit? It is not until the effect of the conceived embryo, in the development of the fetus, that it becomes a male or remains as a female, by either the male sperm cell or the female sperm cell. We start out as female for some time during our pre-birth. Then how can we not share so many similarities than differences? In fact, since we all start out as female in the womb, the correct narrative should be that the word "man" comes from "woman," not the other way around.

We have to genuinely accept the truth of this matter. We have to drop our egos, our entitled arrogance, our fake machismo, and our pre-programmed false way of thinking to truly see each other as the same. There's no harm or fear in that. It is quite the opposite in fact. The minute we are able to accept it, we freely open ourselves up to having a meaningful form of communication and discourse, which then further reveals how much more we have in common. Whenever people open up to each, regardless if it is men with women, just the psychological state of being open with someone makes for a fruitful discussion of sharing meaningful and revealing thoughts.

Just imagine for a minute if men never thought of women as women. In other words, if we somehow lived in a world where men viewed women simply as people, not any type of objectified, sexualized version of this person, but just simply as another person. In this world, men would still have the normal attraction that leads to a relationship and a family, but that attraction would never be at the fore front. A woman's natural attraction would simply be seen as one of the many beautiful aspects of a woman's life, not as the primary one for men. Just from that altered perception of another person, the dynamics of the men/women discussion would completely change for the better, a change borne of true equality and the complete destruction of hierarchical thinking. Even though this alternate world seems implausible, it's actually very plausible. It starts with one person's complete commitment to permanently changing his perception of the opposite sex.

Just like I discussed in the prior Stages of treating every new person in your life with love and curiosity instead of fear and closed-mindedness, we should be able to completely change our understanding and perception of a person of the opposite sex to one where that person is not any different than in us in any way. It is a difficult feat to alter thousands of years of pre-programming, but the human mind is able to grasp such a feat. On an intellectual level, the notion of men being able to appreciate the beauty and artistry of the female form within a non-sexualized perspective while simultaneously viewing women as nothing less than their true equals is possible and plausible. However, thousands of years of pre-programmed archaic and hierarchical precedents have made this reality almost impossible.

Allow me to demonstrate further how much we are the same. Outside of two major physiological and biological differences, which further comprise sub-differences (if you will) from these two, there are no differences between men and women. The biological difference of our reproductive organs is self-explanatory, which results in the corresponding additional biological differences thereof. The other major difference, which not too many people are aware, is that a male's brain is about 10% larger than a female brain. However, this difference is negligible because it has no impact on intelligence whatsoever. In this case, size does *not* matter. Male and female brains are much more alike than different. Other than the size and the inferior-parietal lobule of a man's brain being slightly thicker (again not of much consequence), our brains are the same. If our brains are the same, and they control 100% of all life's actions, does it not come to reason that *we* are the same? Our obvious biological difference notwithstanding, what's left?

I'll tell you what's left. Nothing more than our false perceptions and perspectives of the opposite sex are left. Someone wrote at one time that men are from a certain planet and that women are from a different planet, and therefore they are different in many ways. While I'm not discounting the ideas behind that premise, which I'll explain specifically, I definitely don't agree with the embellished and hyperbolized statement that we're from different planets. Clearly we're from the same planet, the same womb, and the same initial type of fetus. The long-held (false) notion that men and women are different is the premise behind the hyperbole of us being *so* dramatically different that we must be from different planets. While that may be entertaining (arguably) on the surface, it is simply not the case.

There is some truth in the theme behind this idea. That is, that our thinking process differs a bit. Simply put, women are much better at simultaneously utilizing both their left and right hemispheres of the brain than men. This is the main reason for our different ways of thinking. Men tend to remain in the lobe of the brain they are utilizing in the moment of analysis and decision-making. Once they're done in that lobe, then they feel free to cross over to the other lobe. Women tend to freely cross back and forth between these two hemispheres. That's really the only other main difference between us. And if someone wants to use this minor difference as the over-arching (antiquated) argument that we are clearly different, then be my guest. You are just closing yourself off to the many beautiful similarities that we share.

Of the two ways of thinking, I would choose the female brain that can easily go back and forth between lobes. This type of thought process allows for multi-tasking, multi-dimensional analyses, and an awareness of all aspects and contingencies of the thought process. It's like an automatic and inherent pro-and-con list, if you will. It creates and allows for anticipatory preparedness. In other words, you are always many steps ahead in your thinking. I couldn't tell you if my brain is actually physically doing this, but I can tell you that this is how I think. I think on a multi-dimensional basis in which I try to incorporate every possible and foreseeable aspect. By thinking in this manner, I always feel prepared knowing that I've covered every aspect and contingency of the matter in question, so as not to be blindsided by something I had not considered. To me, that just makes better sense.

Now this next position of mine will create even further heated debate and controversy. But when it comes to the ridiculous argument of which sex is better/stronger than the other, which should never be discussed in the first place, I would say that women are better/stronger than men, no question. Again, we shouldn't even be having this argument because it serves no purpose and is ridiculous. I feel like it needs to be addressed if only to help men become more self-aware overall. Men, don't kill me, stay with me here. First, let me say that it's time that men come to terms with this truth and stop being in denial about it. Most men, I believe, actually know this to be true deep down in the depths of their souls.

I had the fortune of being raised by women (my mother, aunt, and older sister). As I indicated previously, my father was a non-entity in my life. He was the worst example of a man. Not only was I raised by women, but I easily had many female friends growing up into my young adulthood. (My wife put an end to those friendships as the first order of business.) Because I was open-minded, observational, and curious, it was easy for me to be friends with women. As a single man in my youth with many friend-girls (not girlfriends), I was able to understand them more than the average guy. In marriage, I had three daughters (now adults), who I raised with my wife. Given my history of being raised by women and having them throughout my life in various forms, I'd like to think that I have an inkling, a smidge of an understanding of a woman's mind. That morsel was enough to help me see the truth of the matter, which is that women are simply better than men at handling and managing life, which makes them the stronger gender.

For thousands of years, women have managed our lives, meaning they take care of everyone beyond just themselves. You have to have great strength and mental fortitude for this task alone. They are the CEOs of life's daily processes and management, in addition to the CEOs of companies. There have been many civilizations in human history that were matriarchal in structure, not the patriarchal civilizations of today. Many animals also live in matriarchal-based family structures. In fact, I would postulate that our world and lives would be much better and different if our modern civilizations were matriarchal in structure. Because women have natural instincts of empathy and care for everyone beyond just themselves, they always care for and nurture everyone without fail and forethought. Their innate concern is to love and care, not destroy and conquer.

More than that, their pattern of thinking is based on compromise and a win-win objective. For them, it makes sense for everyone to win. They view the world this way as opposed to an adversarial way. There doesn't have to be a winner and loser. They see the communal approach as a sensible compromise that appeases and provides for everyone as winners. They value human life and the sanctity of human life. In fact, they place the sacrifice of their own life before that of another. Women are literally the only ones *bringing* new life into the world, not men. When you're able to bring life into a world, you have a greater awareness and love *for* life and *of* life. Let me go further. The person who is literally bringing life into this world is the *only* one who has the ultimate and final say on matters of life. For a man to contribute to the creation of life by only with his sperm (as opposed to physically creating, then delivering it to existence), this is not enough for man to be able to embrace and understand a woman's perspective on life. Therefore, logic dictates that if women are more compassionate, compromising, and win-win in their thought process, a world run by women would be one with no wars and no atrocities against people. How can we argue against such a world?

I would happily live in such a world. At worst, I don't think it could ever be as bad as *"man"* has made it in our current world. Other than the obvious argument that men are physically bigger and stronger than women (because of higher testosterone levels) and are arguably better at handling the more physical and labor-intensive aspects of life, women are the better, stronger sex of the two. Women's mental and psychological state of mind is stronger and more adept at handling adversity, trauma, and challenging situations. It had to be, for child-bearing reasons, and for the responsibility of the welfare of others.

I challenge any man to even conceive the thought of giving childbirth. This thought scares every man. It is unfortunate that men will never know what that feels like or even be able to grasp the concept of the incredible mental and physical strength that it takes to be pregnant with life and give birth to life, let alone the responsibility of caring for that child afterwards. We all take this most important aspect of life as a simple given and for granted. If men were to somehow feel and convincingly intellectualize this enormity that only women experience, I believe that this enlightened awareness alone would alter the way men view women and the world.

Consequently, a man doesn't even have a platform to make an argument about his gender being better than a woman. As they say in a courtroom, you need proper standing to bring a case. Men do not have any standing in court as a party to this proceeding…case dismissed. Next on the docket please.

The Male/Female Dynamic

I've mentioned before how if men viewed women differently, as nothing more than a person of equal footing, 99% of the dynamics between males and females would not exist. But because that's clearly not the case, a discussion is warranted of these dynamics. Sadly, most of the dynamics have been created by men because of their long-held view of superiority over women and women as property. Even in our modern day with all of our achievements and advancements in first-world democratic nations, men still view women within a misogynistic perspective as sexual beings, property, and second class citizens. There are also antiquated laws still in existence that continue to perpetuate the oppression of women. It is truly unbelievable.

Even in the most professional environment where a woman, on paper, allegedly has equal footing, it is not the case behind the scenes. When you turn off the mic, close the doors, and make sure a woman is far enough away from ear shot, what men say about women behind closed doors is reprehensible. I'm not going to cite examples. The worst part is that it's viewed as normal, casual, and not a big deal for men. It is simply viewed as harmless locker room talk. It happens all the time and it happens everywhere, constantly, and without fail. It's suffocating to even think about.

Let me dispel and dismantle this false rhetoric of "locker room" talk right now. That inherently assumes that it's somehow ok as long as it stays in the locker room, which further assumes that it's ok for it to belong there in the first place. We need to completely disallow and destroy any type of trite reference or discussion that downplays and undermines the severity of these horrible words and views of women. When I say we, I mean men, good men, need to call out these misogynists all the time and every time. We need to make sure no one ever deflects and shifts the blame onto women when we call men out on their misogyny. They have to be held accountable and forced into a tight, inescapable corner of being called out, all the time and every time.

I'm not saying all this simply because I have three daughters and no sons. I've felt this way since a young age. I was raised by women, so I grew up with an immediate high level of respect and appreciation for women, as it should be. If I had the good fortune of having sons, I would've ingrained in them since birth these views and positions. By toddler age, they would know what it means to be a highly respectable, decent, upstanding man and human being, one that views everyone with love and equal footing, especially women. During their formative teenage years, I would not only model good male behavior, but I would watch their behavior like a hawk and monitor their every move. I would call them out when necessary and give them the tongue-lashing they might deserve. Unfortunately, many fathers, even today, high-five their sons when they observe a typical misogynistic gesture made by the son. This is despicable modeling behavior.

In the raising of my daughters, I never hid how horrible many men could be. They've known this from a young age. They have all grown to be intellectual adults with full awareness. They know that the second they are remotely disrespected by a man, even in the slightest, to immediately face him in that moment and call him out on his inappropriate disrespect. They were taught not to allow themselves to be victimized in any way and not allow for that behavior to occur even a second time.

I started out this discussion of dynamics by purposely illustrating all the negative aspects of it, to get them out of the way first. Unfortunately, it is mostly because of the thousands of years of negative-based behavior of men that form most of the modern-day dynamics. When it comes to the male/female courting process, men have arrogantly inserted themselves in the position of believing that *they* are the ones "chasing" women. They have created this warped dynamic, and women smartly just play along and use it to their advantage.

Self-aware men know that women ultimately hold all the power and control in the male/female dynamic. These self-aware men allow women to dictate the course of the courting process. Sadly, these men are the minority. The majority of men seem to consistently force the issue with women. They don't have the understanding to take things slow or just simply allow the woman to dictate the flow of the process. They're not adept at reading hints or they simply ignore them when a woman is clearly not interested. They continue to pursue because their ego and arrogance blinds them to the truth of the situation. In many cases, these ego-maniacal men mistakenly take the hints of "get lost" as false signs of encouragement to continue. What?? Ok, good luck with that.

As a man, it saddens me to know how most men are when it comes to the dynamics of the male/female courting process. If I was the world's president on this one particular aspect of life, I would simply tell all men to stop, just literally stop everything. Don't do anything. Just don't. All you have to do is wait and be mildly patient. Allow the woman to approach you first. I've never understood nor agreed with the concept of a man making the first move of any kind. For me, it just made much more sense to approach a woman who has already first clearly shown interest in me. Even then, I usually have to confirm that she truly has interest in me before I decide to cautiously proceed. When I do finally proceed, I make sure to stay mostly quiet so that she's doing most of the talking. This way I learn many things about her as quickly as possible. I ask her questions about herself to show that I care about who she is and what she has to offer to the world. It's not a game or an act. I genuinely care. Women are perceptive to spot a "game." Because I have genuine interest in her as a person first, I listen and ask follow-up questions that show I've been listening.

One day hopefully, when women decide to, maybe they'll completely change and subvert these dynamics to push men where they belong, back on their heels. Only on their heels will they be forced into a situation to actually start thinking about their actions, perspectives, and antiquated world views of women. However, I have a feeling that women won't want to give up this one advantage they possess in our patriarchal dominant structure. They hold the power and control of 100% of all the male/female dynamics of relationships. I just hope that more and more women, who may lack the confidence and self-esteem needed to become aware of their power, value, and worth, will quickly learn that they have the clear advantage and start turning the tables of their failed relationships.

Men need to discard the false male/female dynamic that they've formed. They need to become more self-aware and open-minded. As a man, you just have to face the fact that a woman is better and stronger than you and that she holds all the power. The sooner you do, the sooner you'll have it easier in finding the perfect mate (she'll actually find you and make you think you found her). She will help you become the better man and person that you deserve to be.

"We hold these truths to be self-evident:
that all men **and women** *are created equal."*

ELIZABETH CADY STANTON

REAL, Effective, and Efficient Communication (Words are Everything)

The way you say anything is the way you say everything. Words are absolutely everything! They can make you, they can break you, they can hurt you, they can influence you, and they can carry large-scale destruction on people.

When used properly and effectively, words can be the most amazing, uplifting, and inspirational stimulants to our souls. Humans are social creatures who rely on the company of others. Our human social connections are formed by using words to link us and bond us in ways that would be impossible if we didn't have these words. Words allow us to communicate on deeper levels and create meaningful relationships with others as a result. So why is it so hard sometimes to communicate effectively with one another, particularly if we share opposing views?

Before we get to the fun stuff of dissecting communication failings, I'd like to share with you my love and appreciation of words. As an immigrant to the U.S. at a formative age of seven, I did not know a word of English. I immediately felt the pressure of being a non-English speaking foreigner in elementary school. This was at a time when bullying by kids was part and parcel of a kid's life. To minimize and avoid getting bullied, my survival instincts kicked in, and I immediately realized that I had to learn the language as quickly as possible. Not only that, I had to speak it perfectly and unaccented, and I had to look and sound like the rest of the kids. In other words, I felt I had to assimilate and blend in as quickly as possible so as not to stick out as a target for bullies. I figured out the best and fastest way was to buy a dictionary and literally keep it at my side at all times. Every single time I did not know a word, I would look it up. I watched a ton of television (Gilligan's Island repeats and Three's Company were my go-to shows) to help me learn the language quickly. Within just a matter of literally about two to three weeks, I was speaking and blending in like everyone else, no problem.

As a foreigner and young kid, I learned the value and power of words. I began to love words, everything about them, their roots, their history, everything. Although there were many facets of the English language and its rules that were illogical and made no sense, I accepted them and moved on. I held my dictionary like it was my bible, with pride and respect. Other kids made fun of me and tried to bully me for constantly carrying a large dictionary around. I used my newly-found words to tell them to back off. They never bothered me again, simply because I used the right words with conviction, confidence, and influence. I learned how powerful words can be. Words became my first friends before I could start making friends. To this day, I still have dictionary.com on my phone and computer, and I refer to it regularly. I absolutely love and adore words!

People have historically communicated in person (face to face) for the vast majority of our human existence. It is utterly surreal to think that the preceding thousands of years of human communication have dramatically and overwhelmingly changed in the very recent modern history with the explosion and proliferation of technology. Modern technologies have created significant life-altering ways of new communication methods never before seen in our history. Telephonic, digital, online, and virtual technologies have completely transformed the way we speak and communicate with one another. Nevertheless, the core of effective communication remains the same, regardless of the technological means being used. We still have to be able to convey our thoughts through words that accurately and effectively reflect our meanings and intentions.

Real and effective communication begins when one chooses his/her words wisely and efficiently to convey the precise desired meaning without misunderstanding and ambiguity. Easier said than done, right? Humans don't speak in clear, concise, and unambiguous ways because their minds are going a mile a minute, not to mention we were never taught effective communication. The biggest culprit to not communicating clearly is that when we are talking, we are not actively processing our thoughts into the needed, specific, and precise words of choice. In other words, we're both in a hurry and too lazy to transform our thoughts to the necessary words and choice of words. We leave out additional words and therefore create too much subtext, leading to misunderstanding, miscommunication, and ambiguity. When we think we're trying to be clear, we still forget to include important explanatory words. These words of context and explanation are key to effective communication.

When speaking in person, our body language, facial expressions, and hand/arm gestures typically convey and enhance what our words may not be saying. In other words, the biggest advantage when speaking face to face is that even when we're not effectively

choosing and using the right words or enough of them, this ineffi-
ciency in communication is made up through our body language, to
a large extent. If that fails, the other person typically interrupts you
during the normal flow of conversation to clarify or confirm a point.
However, in today's digital and virtual worlds, what you write in
a textual format inevitably lacks the proper explanation of subtext,
lacks proper connotation, and leaves open too many variables to be
misinterpreted by the other person. This will obviously and inevitably create misunderstandings and miscommunication, sometimes in
ways where the parties get angry and frustrated for no reason.

Why is it so difficult to communicate effectively and efficiently
without misunderstandings and miscommunication? After all, aren't
there more than enough words in our language to precisely express
our thoughts? Well, the supply of words isn't the problem. Proper
communication is always a function of the people involved. Every
person has a different style of communicating, not to mention a different personality that influences their style of speaking and writing.
In addition, the agendas of the people involved, both known and
hidden, influence the manner of communication. Words matter and
word choice matters. Additionally, the efficient use of the chosen
words matters as well.

Most people don't value the use of the proper word to convey
the exact intended meaning. They're in a hurry to speak and/or to
express their thoughts such that they're not actively aware of their
word choice or lack thereof. For some, it's just plain difficult for
them to express themselves, especially if they're not speaking in
their native language. Even when proper words are used, there is
still poor communication because the other side of this problem is
that people don't listen properly either. They're not actively listening when a person is speaking and therefore not comprehending the
conveyed thoughts properly. A lot of us are more focused on speaking and therefore lack the attention required for proper listening and

understanding. Often times, a person is merely looking at the other person talking and thinking about what they're going to say instead of absorbing what the person is saying. It's sad but true.

There is certainly an art to listening, as there is to communicating. Once you master the art of listening, you immediately improve your communication skills by default. To be a great communicator, you have to be a great listener first. When you're actively and intently listening to someone, you're tapping in to your empathy and sympathy. You're naturally able to place yourself in the other person's position. When you do this, you want to understand the other side instead of ignoring them or stopping them so you can speak. The more you listen, the more you learn about people and the more you begin to understand the lives of others. This empathic perspective and approach helps you lower your ego so you can be a better sounding board for a person.

When you practice active listening, you realize that you don't have to say much in return. More importantly, you realize that when you do speak, you do so to provide a meaningful response to that person that helps them more than it does you. You also find that you start actively choosing your words in a methodical manner because you place a higher importance on making sure your thoughts are conveyed properly and succinctly. Over time, the repetitive practice of listening first, then efficiently responding cultivates a successful method of communicating, one without misunderstandings and miscommunication. It leaves the other party feeling like they've been truly heard and appreciated.

Being a better listener definitely makes you a better communicator. Being a better communicator makes you a better person. Other people gravitate towards you, start talking to you more, and seek your advice because they know that you value their time and their concerns. Your better communication skills make others feel validated and important. Most people underestimate the power of words and the art of communication. Becoming both a strong listener and an effective communicator are just as important in your growth towards self-awareness and self-actualization as all the other facets of growth and development. Many people who are focused on improving themselves overlook this aspect of their lives, not realizing that improvements in listening and communicating filter through to other aspects of their lives.

How do you improve upon your listening and communication skills? You start by listening first, as I've described. Drop your ego and stop talking. Stop focusing on yourself when talking and start realizing that people are turned off when you speak about yourself too much. Whenever someone says something about themselves, destroy your impulse to change the subject to you. In fact, every time you talk to someone from here out, particularly if it's for the first time, don't say anything about yourself at all. Just focus on the other person and listen intently on what they're saying and who they are. The only time you should be saying anything about yourself is if you're asked a direct question by that person that requires your specific answer. If that happens, answer it quickly and turn the focus of discussion back on them. This practice and habit will eliminate your ego-centric desire to have to speak all the time, this need to be heard.

Before you know it, you've become an empathetic listener, and you find that you no longer have the need to speak about yourself, let alone speak much at all. As I've said before, there's so much more that you can learn and observe WHEN you're not talking. Your silence speaks volumes. Respect the other person, respect that they're the ones talking, respect your silence, and respond accordingly, but only if and when needed. When you do respond, remember that the words you speak build the house you live in. The way you respond with empathy and efficiently chosen words will not only speak to your character, but it will influence the other person to improve their communication as well.

When you're silent and actively listening to literally every word, what you will also begin to realize is that when people are talking, they are not usually communicating effectively themselves. They're not using proper word choice, they're not using enough explanatory words, they're not reducing the effect of subtext, and they're not properly referring to the subjects of their topic (i.e. misusing pronouns and/or not using specific identifying words). Because you've become a great listener, you understand what they're trying to convey regardless of their poor communication. Your awareness on a subtextual level is greatly enhanced. You'll find that if you don't understand, you will politely chime in to simply clarify the point being made and allow them to continue. You ultimately become a master wordsmith and a clear expresser of your thoughts. This becomes second nature to you, all because you started by being a better active listener.

In my prior professions, I've had the fortune of being in a position where clear and effective communication (verbal and written) was of the highest importance. Over time, I gained the technical and tactical skills of effective, concise, and precise writing and communicating. This was an environment in which I worked with transactional attorneys on a daily basis, thereby placing greater importance on written skills and communication skills. Transactional attorneys are the conduits that allow for business transactions between two parties to occur seamlessly and effectively in a win-win scenario for both parties. These are the attorneys whose art of putting words together in a contract allow for business to be conducted. The contracts, agreements, and documents that they create have to be specific, clear, logical, unambiguous, all-inclusive, and account for every single contingency and the contingencies of the original contingencies. Every detail is accounted for in these documents. They are written in a logical and methodical order with defined terms, to make certain that the reader would never be confused or question any detail.

For me, working in this environment for two decades taught me how to think, write, and communicate logically and effectively, using fewer words than necessary as to be concise. This experience has literally and permanently re-programmed my brain to a method of thinking about anything and everything in a much more orderly, logical fashion. If you've never worked in an environment where thinking, writing, and communicating in the most efficient manner was the main priority, may I suggest that the next time you come across a legal contract or agreement of any time, spend the mundane few minutes and actually read through this document. Although it may seem foolish and cumbersome, you'll find that the words used and the manners in which they are used actually make the most sense. You'll begin to understand why choosing the right words, using identifying words, referring to the proper subjects, etc. is important in improving your communications skills. You'll start to think in a more logical, clear manner and you'll be able to formulate and convey your thoughts more effectively.

To additionally help you in your quest of becoming a strong communicator, the following basic guidelines and tools are important to incorporate in your daily practice of listening and communicating. The following also assumes that you are actively listening in the communication process.

1. Context is everything. We live in a high context society. First, you have to clearly understand your own context as well as the other person's context. You have to be on the same contextual page. When you clearly frame your context with proper introductions, explanations, and clarifications, you leave very little to nothing for subtext, which is the goal. The more subtext you allow devoid of context, the more of a chance of misunder-

standing and miscommunication. For example, how often do you see a social media post with no context whatsoever? Or how often does a friend call/text you and immediately starts communicating in what seems to be the middle of a conversation of which you were never a participant. It's frustrating and annoying because you don't understand the message or the reason. You have to be a detective and piece together the message. Properly framing your context first is key to the start of proper communication.

2. Try your best to always have a clean slate of mind before starting a communication. Leave your assumptions by the way side and do not have any preconceived notions or ideas of the subject matter. Nor should you have any default judgments, biases, or agendas. Always take people at face value and give them every benefit of the doubt. Meet people where they are in their style of language and communication. Do not chime in by ending their sentences for them. You may be on the wrong path. It is very difficult and challenging to achieve a completely clean state of mind without any type of harmless bias, but the more you practice this method, the easier it will become. You'll become a better listener in the process, one that will never feel the urge to finish someone's sentence.

3. Be aware of when either you or the other person is not clearly articulating the thoughts in our heads. Often times, people will have a certain thought but when they begin talking, they don't immediately realize that they're not actually communicating the thought in their head. In other words, they think they said one thing, but really they said something else. Usually it's because they leave out a critical word or two, or not use the more precise word in that moment. They might get angry and frustrated at you for not understanding them when they are the

ones not clearly explaining. When that happens, it's important to pause and reset the conversation. You can do that kindly and diplomatically by simply saying, "ok, let me see if I got this right…" or something similar.

4. Do not assume that you understand the message from the other person the way you think you are. In other words, the moment you begin to question yourself, or you stop paying attention because you're trying harder to understand, or you notice the other person has a quizzical look on their face, stop and clarify in that very moment. There's no reason why a misunderstanding has to occur or grow. Stop the communication flow and re-direct it in real time.

5. Communication when you're on the same page is hard enough, but when you are discussing and debating opposing views, that becomes even more difficult and complicated. Respectful discourse can easily go by the wayside when discussing politics, religion, or any controversial issue, particularly when the parties are on opposite ends of the spectrum. I don't need to remind you that everyone is entitled to their opinion on these serious topics. In fact, the more serious the topic, the more someone's opinion should be valued and respected. When that level of respect serves as the baseline and framework by both parties (as it should), an intelligent and productive discussion/debate can take place, one where both sides are free to and are allowed to express their opinions. Anger and frustration, which can lead to potentially insulting comments, serve no purpose when it's difficult to curb your emotions and convictions. Conversely, the calmer and more composed you are in your demeanor, the more effective and erudite your opinions come across. The best advice I can give you to quell your emotions and focus at the issue at hand is simply just that. Stay focused on the actual

issues and arguments. Don't stray into judgments and insults. Debate the issue as if you're in a game. In a sporting game, each side always has an unfettered and unbiased opportunity to try to score (make a point). So if you treat the discussion as a fair game of wits, you'll find the debate to be enjoyable and fun instead of adversarial and wasteful.

6. Regarding politics in particular, almost every discussion can become heated. This is the case because people argue the label on the other side instead of the person. A person's political party becomes the target instead of discussing the issue on its merits. People get focused and sidetracked by labels and affiliations instead of who they really are and what they really stand for. They get amped up by the mere label of someone before they even start any type of discourse. They're stuck in the "judging the book by its cover" mentality. The best advice I can give to avoid a freefall of debasing barbs in this situation is to realize that not every opinion, position, or thought is political and/or should be politicized. In other words, NOT everything is a political statement and NOT everything should be politicized. You have to differentiate opinions and positions from it merely and solely being a political statement. For example, if you were to make a comment on only the character of a candidate, that shouldn't be viewed as a party line comment; it is nothing more than a comment on the character at face value. It is a comment that should stand on its own without any skewing by a party line. You may not be happy or in agreement by this comment, but it shouldn't be viewed as a political statement. More importantly, you have to disregard in your mind the label (the party) of the person from whom the opinion is made. For example, if neither of you is made aware of each other's party designation, you would both be much more open and receiving of the other's comment, simply because you're not influenced

or misdirected by the party affiliation. The moment the party affiliation becomes known, your whole psychology changes, for the worst, and it shouldn't. You immediately view the other person as an adversary instead of just a person.

7.   When communicating digitally through a textual format, the above rules become even more significant because there is more contextual framing needed in order for the other person to fully understand your point. You have to remember that there is no emotional connotation attached to your text. You have to not only frame the context of the message, but you have to frame your emotional state. You have to describe the connotation of the words you are using; otherwise the other person will fill in that connotation, which often times is wrong. The use of emojis and emoticons actually helps to frame the emotions of the dialogue. Since they are more prevalent in today's digital format and are more utilized, the correct connotations of the text exchanges have become more common as well.

8.   In any form of digital/textual communication where you don't see the other person, proper use of grammar and punctuation is also very important. Meanings are completely altered when incorrect grammar and punctuation are a factor. Typos are also horrible speed bumps that break the flow of communicating. Proofreading your texts before sending is a must. After sending a text/message, you should also catch and correct typos, wrong word choice, and incorrect grammar/punctuation by sending a follow-up revised text/message. These corrections should be done as immediately as possible after the sent text. Consistent and persistent proofreading and correcting should be an automatic, involuntary aspect of your digital communication.

9. An important point on proper etiquette of digital/textual communication is that you should respond to the person immediately, if not as soon as possible, particularly if you're the one who started the text thread in the first place. How often have you been texted by another person and respond to them immediately only for them to take the whole day to respond back? How rude is that? When having an actual back-and-forth conversation via text, it is rude and improper to leave the other person hanging. There are certainly times when immediate responses are not needed, and sometimes no response is needed. These are obvious situations in which the other person is clearly aware. However, an actual conversation is not one of them. At a minimum, you should have a simple response that states you'll get back to them shortly, to give you a moment.

10. Lastly, the following consideration applies to both in-person communication and digital: don't just text me, subtext me. In other words, speak to me for real, in the real. What I mean by this is that subtext is the most crucial component of communication because within subtext is where the truth lies. So don't just say words that don't mean anything or are false in nature. Speak the truth to me. Expose the subtext of our dialogue. Live in the REAL! It makes for easier communication.

"When you talk, you are repeating what you already know. But if you listen, you may learn something new."

THE DALAI LAMA

STAGE 16:

Your Personal Growth

Personal growth is such a general statement. Simply stated, if you're not becoming a better person every day of your life, then what are you doing? If you want a better life, you have to become a better person. It's that simple really. What are you doing in your life then, if not trying to better yourself?

You have to start taking the small steps towards the vision of growth by becoming smarter, stronger, more mature, more self-aware, more emotionally intelligent, seeking more knowledge, seeking and identifying the meanings in your life, and ultimately gaining the wisdom to start living a self-actualized life. Let's just start this journey then already. Why not now? What's holding you back? Shed any masks that have been your crutch thus far. You won't need them anymore. All you'll need is the shovel in your mind to start digging deep into your heart, mind, and soul. In those places, you will find all the answers. They're all there just waiting for you.

The goal of continued and consistent personal growth should begin the moment you become rationally aware of your human existence in a profound and meaningful way. If that hasn't happened yet, I can understand not striving to be better. But if you're even scratching at the realization that your life is precious and that you want to live and be your authentic true self, then let's get to it.

The first important step is to simply understand that this will be a permanent approach to your life. There are no finite answers to life. You'll always be growing, morphing, self-evaluating, self-revealing, broadening your awareness, and shedding layers of yourself. This will be an amazing and life-affirming path of discovery and projection into the person you will become. At the beginning, you have to de-construct yourself. You have to un-define and unburden yourself from the constructs of society, your history, your environment, and everything else in your life that hasn't allowed for personal growth. You have to reconstruct your life in a way where you surround yourself with all the opportunities and open pathways of allowing growth.

Just like flowers need water for growth and blooming, you'll have to completely open yourself to allow water to penetrate you deep enough into every crevice of your soul. This reconstruction will fuel the blooming of your personal growth. Just like a caterpillar unknowingly sheds its skin and morphs into a new and beautiful butterfly, you will have the needed faith in the unknown at the beginning of your journey. You will need this internal faith to continue to guide you by what sets your soul on fire. The outcome is a creature in the form of a beautiful and authentic you.

Once you start on your path and allow yourself to be open, you'll find that there are endless resources (beyond the constructs that you just destroyed) that will appear to you to help you and corroborate for you that you're on the right path. Now that the prior constructs of life are not in your way anymore, like-minded information, books, and people will start to fill your world and create an additional support system for you. The key is to always be open to the information, but at the same time, question this information in penetrating ways to continue to arrive at the truths you've been incorporating in your life.

Now that you're using your diagnostic mind more consistently, you will be asking questions regularly and you'll be able to arrive at the correct answers yourself. Keep fighting the easy, reactive part of your mind every time you get a little discouraged or feel like you're starting to lose a sense of direction. When you fight your reactive mind to stay on track, you force yourself to continue utilizing your diagnostic thinking in creative, imaginative, and revealing ways. This is the way of living life intentionally and with purpose.

One of the goals is to get to this permanent approach to life where you're living it with determined intention and purpose. You're not just floating along; you are determining your course with the necessary mental intention of consistent forethought and analysis. This approach will become a regular pattern, which will become an easy, involuntary of way thinking. You'll find that in almost every minute of your daily routine, you're actually so present in the moment and so clear in your thinking, that it will amaze you at times. That awe and amazement is a tiny miracle that reminds you you're progressing and growing as an evolving person.

This has been my way of thinking for so long that many times, I get a little overwhelmed with the flood of rapid-fire clear thoughts, realizations, and focused direction that my mind is experiencing. It's not the anxiety-inducing type of overwhelming that fosters fear of the unknown; it is a welcomed overwhelming of relief that gives me the answers that I need. I enjoy being overwhelmed by these thoughts and realizations. They are telling me that I'm on the right track in a perceptible and tangible way. It reminds me that life is coming to m*e* and at m*e*, which is the goal. You don't want to be aggressive and forceful in your approach when living your daily life. You want to allow life to come *to* you and *at* you, where you easily and seamlessly absorb every aspect of it.

I call this the rope-a-dope of life, where you dodge and weave against every ebb and flow of life's waves like a light-footed tap dancer. The key is to deflect anxiety's deterrence and convert that feeling into fuel. Whenever you feel anxious or overwhelmed, you have to externalize this feeling into productive, creative, and/or positive action. The moment the anxiety virus starts to invade and corrupt your mind and psyche, you have to re-wire its effect by turning it into fuel. This fuel then converts and externalizes your anxiety into positive and productive action. Consequently, you can use this anxiety as a benefit instead of being defeated and debilitated by it. This is the common feeling of "butterflies in your stomach," where anxiety is reduced to a form of exciting and nervous energy, right before the start of an important event.

For example, athletes naturally feel this way before games and have mastered the use of this nervous energy as fuel for their successful performance, instead of allowing anxiety to deter them. As they say in sports, let the game come to you, don't force it. This is the rope-a-dope of life approach. As you've probably experienced in your life, whenever you try to force something, you inevitably lose all control of it and it doesn't turn out as you had expected, leaving you frustrated and angry. Again, flowing with the water current is better served than flowing against it. Just as water fills and flows consistently into every open space, so will you. Bruce Lee was a master of this metaphor of life. However, you can and you must continue to live your life with intention and purpose. You're still the driver and decider of which outlet you want to flow into. This is how you reconcile the invisible line of letting life come to you while still living it proactively and with meaningful intention. You are balancing on and traversing the tightrope of life in this manner.

I'd like to share a personal example of not forcibly bending life in your direction. When we're driving our car, every time we come to a curve or a turn, we turn the wheel slightly into the change of direction, and our car smoothly and easily follows this change of course. We never over-turn the wheel as far as it can go, or ever even come close to it. Just a slight turn of the wheel of life is all we need. When we do that, the full turn eventually follows in due course. I actually learned this important life lesson both on a literal and figurative level when I was about eight years old. I was at Disneyland about to ride the track car for the first time ever. This is the type of car ride where a track running between the wheels keeps it on course no matter what the driver does. This was also the first time driving any type of kid car for me. My older brother by sixteen years was my passenger. When I came to my first turn, I gripped the wheel firmly with all the might of an eight-year-old and turned the wheel as far as it could go. The car of course slammed against the middle track and came to an instant grind against it, making a raucous noise. In that moment, my brother simply took his left hand, gently placed it on the steering wheel and said, "like this," as he effortlessly gave what to me seemed like the slightest turn of the wheel ever.

In that moment, I literally not only learned how to properly drive this track car, but I also understood the general concept of driving a real car. A year later, I remember actually driving my mom's car at about age nine in a remote area away from other cars. Believe it or not, not only did she foolishly allow me to do that, with her as the passenger, but I was actually *teaching her* how to drive a car so she could pass her upcoming driver's license test. In that prior little moment of what my brother showed me, I not only learned how to drive a car, I also learned a broader approach to life. This approach is to simply make gentle turns in life, not aggressive overpowering ones. I was inspired to expand my way of thinking to a level of subtext, beyond the superficial. I seemed to regularly find more meaning than what was being presented to me in the moment. I began to look for them also. In my English classes at school, for example, this inspiration made it easy for me to find the deeper themes in poems and novels as they were readily apparent to me.

This is how inspiration works. When you're inspired and taught to make a permanent change, that inspiration becomes permanent because belief itself is not enough. Proper inspiration requires belief plus intentional and consistent action that ultimately reprograms your mind and your way of thinking into a habit-forming pattern. This pattern becomes ingrained in your daily routine from the inside out. That's the beauty of inspiration versus motivation. Inspiration forces you to take 100% of the accountability and action-required responsibility. When you do that, it stays with you forever. Motivation, on the other hand, allows a person to blame the motivator because it is human nature to blame others, especially when there could be another to blame (such as a third-party motivator) instead of taking one's own personal accountability.

Motivation only works for a temporary period and requires the same consistent external stimulus outside of yourself to keep motivating you. Motivation is great when you need a coach to give you a boost of confidence to hit the game winning shot. Inspiration keeps you locked in for life. All of the great athletes of our time have the same undeniable trait in common, which is, they are all self-inspired, permanently confident individuals who never needed to rely on anyone other than themselves.

When you're properly inspired and continue to be inspired to make permanent changes, consistent personal growth in your life is the result. It becomes your default approach to life. You wake up every day knowing clearly in your mind that you have to become a better person today than you were yesterday. That methodology and self-inspiration continues for every day of your life. Isn't it refreshing and appealing to know that once you become a better person day after day, you never again have to be any lesser of yourself from that point forward? I love waking up with that awareness every day. You begin to live in your own self-created environment of clarity, recovery, and creativity, where distractions are now meaningless and no longer disrupt your flow. It is akin to a permanent simmer of fire under your big bowl of confidence, and it never runs out of fuel, allowing you to be an early version of your soon-to-be future self.

When you start living your life this way, bringing you closer to your true self, you'll find that you won't feel the need to seek social companionship from people as often, if at all. When a person is not living in their truth, they feel the strong need to be around more people and have more friends. They want to go out more, they want to spend hours and hours on social media scrolling and posting. They want to do everything socially possible in order to not be alone in a room with themselves and their thoughts. Being overly socially involved, especially with people you don't consider true friends, is indicative of living with masks on and denying who you are. Being alone in a room forces you to look at yourself, something that you're not capable of doing. Truths have a way of being more self-evident when you're alone. Surrounding yourself with a superficial social circle, both in person and virtually, keeps you distracted from yourself in a veil of temporary and fake comfort.

When you've started the path of being inspired to change yourself, you naturally find that you're not relying on this superficial social circle any longer. In fact, you start spending more alone time. You long to be alone with the comfort of your own thoughts. This is one of the best signs of personal growth. Being alone and lost in your own thoughts becomes a joy and comfort instead of anxiety and loneliness. Your home becomes more of a sanctuary for you. It becomes a place of self-revelation and self-inspiration. You find that you need to be at home to foster that continued inspiration, without the disturbance of the outside world. Being at home becomes your vacation. You become a tourist in your own life, where you made it your own holiday. You don't feel the need to visit an exotic place for escapism any longer. When you can make where you are your vacation, then you're at peace with yourself in a way that the need to escape no longer exists.

When you visit other places in the world on actual vacations, you don't look at them as vacations any more. You look at them as enjoyable learning experiences of other peoples in other countries. You cherish the time and experiences that you share with these new people. You know that your permanent vacation spot is still where you made it, your home. If you happen to live alone, do not submit to and allow the traditional constructs of society to shame you of living alone. Whether you live alone or in a family setting, it has absolutely no bearing on your personal growth and your trajectory. Societal judgments have no place in your personal ascendancy and transcendence.

Another example of your growth evolution is when you start looking at famous people, highly successful people, and well-known celebrities as nothing more than just regular people. They are simply other humans, no less and no more superior or inferior than you. You are not intimidated by anyone in the slightest, especially people of power who are perceived to be higher than you in status or career position. You know that your level of confidence can easily place you in their "circle", if need be, and that you firmly stand on equal footing with them. You know you can take them on at any level and in any capacity. After all, death is the ultimate equalizer and the ultimate one-size fits all...*memento mori*. At the same time, however, you are humble enough to know that arrogance has no place in any setting with all people in general. Your strong sense of humility and probity knows to welcome and treat people, who others may regard as lower status (even though you don't), with the same respect and equal-footing. Regardless how others view various levels of perceived status, you don't. You see everyone as equals and as humans.

Your growth ascendancy will bring overall balance to your life, always keeping you centered. The ancient Greeks had many philosophies they lived by. One of my favorites was their axiom of "nothing in excess" — three simple yet amazingly powerful words. Nothing in excess is a reminder to live your life in the center or close to it, as balanced as possible. Do not live your life in the extremes. The extremes are where your life goes in the wrong direction, where addictions can overtake you, where you're easily prone to brainwashing, and where you start losing yourself entirely. As a Libra, I absolutely adore this balanced-scale perspective on life. It suits me to a tee.

In Greek mythology, the story of Icarus is a great tale that symbolizes this axiom. Icarus, a mortal man, attempted to fly as high as the sun with his father's man-made wings. Although warned by his father, he arrogantly got too close to the sun, which burned his wings, causing him to come crashing down to his death. His extreme pride made him believe he was an equal with the immortal Greek Gods, a pride that lasted but a short while. Extremes only last but for a short while, however intoxicating that while may be.

With this new sense of balance in your life, you'll be in a position to face the many adversities and challenges that life throws your way. You won't cower in fear from being overwhelmed. You won't get pushed down by the negativities of the moment because you'll be living for the next moment of resolution that follows. You won't have a lack of confidence to debilitate you. You'll rely on your precision mind and your unwavering confidence to forge ahead and find an adequate resolution to the adversity. With every challenge you strike down like a samurai warrior, your resolve grows stronger, and your life becomes easier to manage. You'll also gain a strong conviction that no matter what else life throws at you, it won't ever compare to the worst adversity you've already conquered. What can ever be worse than what you've already faced and resolved? Nothing…because your past adversities have instilled a permanent state of gratitude and gratefulness for all that you have in your life. This serves as a reminder for the next challenge in your life.

More importantly, you're learning from your many mistakes along the way. You're not perfect and never will be. But you become less imperfect by taking complete accountability and responsibility of your mistakes. You make sure you make full amends (never half-hearted) along the way to the people you inadvertently hurt in any minor way. You also focus more on learning from others who've made mistakes, instead of making them yourself, so as to prevent them in the first place. Your keen awareness and observance help you to easily see the mistakes of others from which you learn. This is a higher level of thinking and approach to life.

Although you start to really understand this game of life, you're not foolish enough to think that you are in competition with anyone. Competition resides in the game of sports, not in the game of life. Your one and only point of competition is with yourself in the daily pursuit of being better than yesterday's version of yourself. You realize that the concept of competition with others in any form is lunacy and completely unnecessary. Competition becomes irrelevant when your focus is consistently on your own unique and differentiated value-added you provide to others, and of the genuine service of others. With this approach, you have completely differentiated yourself in such a way that people automatically seek you out because of it. This ends all competition as far as you're concerned. You stand alone and apart from all competition. You obliterate the competition.

"Between stimulus and response, there is a space. In that space is our power to choose our response. In our response lies our growth and our freedom."

VIKTOR FRANKL

"What lies behind us, and what lies before us, are tiny matters compared to what lies within us."

RALPH WALDO EMERSON

The REAL You vs.
The Real World
(A Daily Dilemma)

Mark Twain perfectly said that the two most important days of your life are the day you were born and the day you discover why. I love this statement for so many reasons. Not only does Twain pay tribute to the preciousness and miracle of life, but he also addresses a second day of birth that is just as precious, that of your awakening. Doesn't that statement alone inspire you to discover your second birthday, if you haven't yet? It certainly does for me. The day you discover you're finally living your REAL authentic self is a miracle to behold.

When this happens, you will live freely as your REAL self on a daily basis, which will require regular reconciliation by you with the antagonistic real world that is not in line with your identity and your probity. However, the need for this reconciliation will diminish over time and go away completely once you've figured out how to traverse this non-REAL world. Living your REAL self will become easy and unaffected by the world's contradictions.

The indescribable irony with the real world of today is that this world is anything but a REAL world, right? In other words, it's not what most of us would want the world to be. It's actually not the REAL world, but it's the only one we have, so there is no choice in the matter. Within the title of this Stage, the REAL you, once realized will be in opposition and juxtaposition against the real world, which is not REAL, at least based on my REALogy® philosophy. What will happen and needs to happen is that over time, you will transcend the daily confines of this world and not concern yourself with the judgments, oppositions, and restrictions of this world. They won't matter or affect you anymore. They will become meaningless because you will have reprogrammed your way of thinking. Your new habits and behaviors of living your daily life will render pointless the confines of your prior existence.

In a sense, you will create your own REAL world in this way. This will liberate you because this is when most everything will make complete sense to you. Your life will become the simplest and easiest it has ever been. Your first thought will inevitably be, "why didn't I discover this a long time ago?" There's no better time than the present. In this present, you will be your REAL self 24/7 in your own REAL world.

While you're living in your own REAL world as best as you can make it, your hope for all of humanity will be the same. You will live with this hope but will know intellectually, at the same time, that humanity and civilization in today's governments and politics are not aligned with your growth and new self. Governments are set up in ways that create societal systems that limit, monitor, and minimize your voice and individuality. You'll do your part by voting for the best possible proxy of politicians, but you will do so knowing that your effort to effect real change in the world is still a tiny abrasion of pebbles against the rocky mountains of immovable counter forces. The next best bit of effort on your part is to live your life as freely as possible against these forces and to share your voice with your inner circle of family and close friends, and hopefully with the greater communities beyond them, one person at a time.

Full acceptance, respect, and love of your fellow human being and all of humanity, without reservation, bias, or equivocation, is an absolute necessity for mankind and cannot be questioned or denied. While this isn't quite the world we live in today in which many people and countries are at odds with each other, this everyday approach of unadulterated acceptance of others must hold true for hope to continue to exist and persist. We fail to remember that all we have is each other. When we look at another person who has been labeled as an enemy without any credible merit other than the indoctrinated one ascribed by our government, religion, race, etc., we have failed. Our failure of recognition of another for no other reason than hate is the most egregious affront any human can make against another, shy of premeditated murder and genocide, which is often the next step.

It is so unfathomable and mind-boggling that a person can look at another person and NOT see that we share the same human form, we breathe the same air, we require the same basic needs of sustenance and survival, and we share the same red tinge of our blood, without fail. Our bodies comprise the same organs, tissues, and bones. There is none among our eight billion people on this Earth that differs physiologically in any way. We have the same hearts that pump the same life-sustaining blood coursing our same veins.

The only differences that we have are the opposing thoughts that penetrate our minds without checking in with our hearts first. These are the horrible thoughts that differ in such profound ways that they create irreversible mental prisons. The only solution we see through these mental prisons is the propagating and promulgating of hate, which then matriculates into the most heinous atrocities we could ever commit. If these thoughts were to pause and take a foothold in our hearts first, they may lose their potency by the time they reach our minds. Instead of entering a mind with irreversible prisons, these thoughts now have a chance for analysis in an open floor plan of a mind with no doors and locks. In this open floor plan, differing thoughts have a chance to change. When they're processed through the heart, there's always hope for the mind.

Let me offer a visual example of processing through the heart versus through an indoctrinated mind. If you place a loved dog from a nurturing household in a room full of mirrors, his response to his own reflection will be that of a happy recognition of someone like himself and he'll want to play with that reflection. He'll come out of that room wagging his tail in delight thinking he's made a new friend. If you were to place an unloved dog from a hostile environment in that same room of mirrors, the reflection he will see is that of an enemy that needs to be attacked. His brainwashed mind is incapable of even seeing that the image is him. He'll run out of that room growling in anger trying to hunt down the reflected enemy. Which pooch do you have in your household? Better yet, who do you see when you look in *your* mirror? Are you even looking into your own eyes? Do you see truth in your eyes that forms an involuntary smile of joy on your face? Or are you looking away from your eyes altogether?

I've already made it clear that one of the themes of REALogy® is that we have the immense power of our minds to reprogram the deviated thought patterns of our past and become a new person as a result. If we think with our hearts first, we have a chance to change these horrible ingrained thought patterns. Imagine if the people who see themselves as violent adversaries of each other simply decided to be remotely influenced by their loving hearts. They would wake up one day with thoughts and minds changed to full acceptance of enemies no longer. That's really all it takes, right? Just flip a switch and realize that the sinister ways of the centuries-old past were NOT the right ways. Those were the wrong paths of life. The right paths are wide open for their new journeys. All they need to do is fight off the much greater voices in their minds of thousands of years of deep-rooted hatred. What a life-defining moment that would be. Many might say it would be a miracle. It so happens that I believe in miracles and I am witness to them. I hope there are more of us who believe in such powerful miracles.

When you have righted your life and are living your best true self, it can become overwhelming when you start carrying the burdens of the rest of humanity. As a self-actualized person living in the REAL, you become so much more empathic of your fellow man that the burden of caring for others can make you feel hopeless and defeated. You take on the responsibilities of healing the world and solving all the ills of our daily lives that it becomes discouraging. This is a difficult perspective to manage, it truly is. On the one hand, you are feeling the unending joy of heart and peace of mind by living your authentic life; but it is a life tempered by your knowledge that others are suffering and that not much can be done. I honestly don't have too many solutions to offer other than to continue treating every person with kindness and acceptance while conveying this truth onto others along the way.

For me, writing this book and expressing my thoughts on the matter is where I felt I had to go. My core desire of helping people was the DNA and genesis of this book. It became my genuine mission. This is my way of helping people on a broader scale, hopefully reaching as many as possible. You will also find your vehicle of expression in some way. Your core beliefs and hopes have to permanently serve as the fuel that blazes your soul on fire. Those passions of fire must remain undying in the face of the harshest winds and hurricanes. Your heart, soul, and mind have to be protected daily from these elements by the impenetrable armor of hope that you've so skillfully welded for yourself. If not you and me, the ones who care, then who will?

Charles Bukowski once said, "The problem with the world is that the intelligent people are full of doubts, while the stupid ones are full of confidence." I have a friend with whom we share our recurring discussion of the world's problems. Every time without fail, at the end or our discussion right before he leaves, he turns to me and the last thing he always says to me is, "Ok Ark, I'm leaving you in charge now!" It's funny, but I've found that I've taken on that persona. I feel like there's a big part of me that owes it to the world to help it in the best way I know how. I'm glad that I feel this way. I've always felt this way and I remember having the feeling of wanting to help people throughout my life. I've found great joy in being helpful, offering advice, doing favors, and being in service of others. I'm consistently doing that today. I literally leverage every skill, knowledge, experience, and resource that I have to help others. I'm the go-to person for all my family and friends, their trusted advisor if you will.

I owe that sense of communal spirit and courage to my mother. I owe most everything to her in fact. She was an amazingly strong woman who tried to defy her odds and make a new life for her, myself, and the rest of our family. Before we immigrated to America, my mother was a manager, fashion designer, and seamstress of a clothing factory in the communist Soviet Union. The fact alone that she was a working woman in a communist nation was impressive, but she was also a career-driven woman. She brought that strength and spirit with her when we came to America, the new world of hope and opportunity for us. She had an entrepreneurial spirit (which I also inherited), so she decided to open her own women's dress-making boutique as a fashion designer. Because she was still new to the American ways of capitalism and business, she hadn't yet acclimated from the drastic departure of the communist ways. She was fierce and tried her hardest to make her business successful, but she ultimately failed and had to close her boutique. Or at least she thought she failed by American standards. This was so devastating for her that it proved to be her mental breaking point after the many years of hardships, adversities, and trauma she had lived through leading up to this devastation in her life. She lost hope and she lost her courage. When courage is lost, your self-worth is lost. When self-worth is lost, all is lost.

She fell into deep depression, which sadly turned into paranoid schizophrenia. I was about twelve years old at the time. I remember feeling a tremendous amount of guilt for not being able to help her save, manage, and make her business successful. I believed that my twelve-year-old brain should've had the business knowledge to help her. I also felt guilt for the massive mental breakdown that she had as a result, which robbed her of over fifteen years of her life before finding peace again. I still feel a bit of guilt to this day. I took that guilt, along with her strength and entrepreneurial spirit, and forged a path in my life where I vowed to live the life that she had fought so hard to manifest for herself and our family.

My mother was my first example of someone who defied and denied her history and her societal restrictions and expectations in a backwards country. She was determined to be how she truly saw herself. She saw her vision, in a new country of opportunity, and blasted straight ahead, unfettered towards it, from point A to B. In her quest for joy in her heart and peace in her mind, she could not overcome the last bit of her perceived failure. Her rocket vision of the beautiful world on the other side of her determined perseverance was permanently cataracted by her breakdown. I took her devastation and made it my own. I never wanted to feel and experience what she went through, both in her professional career and personal life. I learned from her experiences and I vowed to live the life that she wanted for herself. In other words, I learned from my mother to be determined in living the life I envisioned for myself. It took me a few years to gain the strength and confidence to do so. Over time, I started to shed that fear and leaned firmly on my belief and confidence in myself to venture on without regret, never looking back.

Any time I felt a little less hopeful or discouraged, I remembered what losing hope and courage did to my mom. The sudden loss of power and control of her strong mind under the suppressive and heinous debilitation of mental illness was an iron-branded, permanent mark in my own mind. It was such an undeniable, vibrant, and indelible stamp on my brain. I will never forget the moment that my mother mentally checked out right in front of my young eyes, the moment she unsubscribed from life. I vowed to myself that I would harness the power of my own mind so sharply and potently that the loss of it would never be feasible, possible, or imaginable. There was absolutely no possible way. I simply had to keep my mental acuity as healthy and strong as possible. Thus far I have. I'm truly proud of that achievement, with the full knowledge and awareness that I still have the rest of my life to go.

Maybe her suffering wasn't all for not. Maybe it fortified my resolved perseverance to catapult me to become the person I am today. I am so grateful for that. It lessens the guilt I've carried and I'm hopeful it will completely go away one day. I continue to power on without ever having allowed any of my mistakes and failures throughout my life to stop me in my tracks. I've been resolute in my stinginess of learning from all the many lessons from every mistake and failure, and vowing never to repeat them. This is the simplest definition and personification of personal growth.

"There is but one cause of human failure.
And that is man's lack of faith in his true Self."

WILLIAM JAMES

"Excellence does not require perfection."

HENRY JAMES

STAGE 18:

Faith, Spirituality, and Religion

Are you a spiritual person? Are you a religious person? Are you both? Neither? There are so many layers of answers to these questions. Ultimately, I believe that it is a simple matter of choice for each individual person. This is a choice that shouldn't be judged, influenced, argued against, contradicted, or opposed. Nor should the person be persecuted, discriminated against, or ostracized by this choice. Acceptance and tolerance are the only responses we should have, if any at all.

Spirituality and religion are incredibly difficult to discuss in almost any format. Volumes and volumes of written materials have been written about these two monumental topics of mankind for thousands of years with widely-ranging and differing opinions. The varying perspectives from hundreds of religions from ancient civilizations to early civilizations and ultimately to our present-day civilization have also contributed to these volumes of writings. I certainly won't be able to render any justice to them from my personal perspectives and opinions on the matter, and certainly not from a small chapter in this book. Nor is it my intention to do so, as I am neither a theologian nor a specific spiritualist.

Personally, spirituality and religion have and continue to play an integral role in my growth and awareness. However, I do not believe that it is a prerequisite for anyone to incorporate in their personal lives. Personal growth does not depend on them. I contemplated not having this section in my book because it does not have to be a Stage in your evolution of the authentic self. I do not want to impose my presumptions onto others in this area. I firmly believe and am completely aware that attaining a higher true self, wisdom, self-actualization, and the ultimate evolution into an overall better person can be done without including spirituality or religion in your life. The only essential belief for a person to hold is genuine belief in yourself, the most important one.

That is the beauty of life. It does not have to be guided by a faith in anything outside of yourself. That is your personal choice. At the same time, having a faith beyond yourself (so long as you always place the self first) is also a choice for someone who *does* want the sense of guidance that reassures oneself. Consequently, I did not want to bypass these significant subjects altogether either. I would simply like to share my personal perspectives and opinions, but merely as a testimonial of my own personal evolution, and not in any way to influence you or convince you of anything on this matter. That is my sole aim.

I believe in the following as they have all played important roles in my life: spirituality, faith in a higher being, religion (in the general sense, not denominational sense), an afterlife of some form, universal cosmic energy, human energy, human connection, and miracles. They have always and consistently supported, nurtured, and guided my authentic identity, my purpose and passions of life, and the paths I've lead. I remember always being a spiritually-based person. Even during the times of my life when I deeply contemplated/questioned the roles of spirituality in my life and whether or not they needed to be a part of my life, I always came back to my personal conclusion that I *want* them in my life. Ever since I began noticing important signs in my life, what I call miracles, I chose to believe in the reasons why they happened to me. I therefore chose to believe in these miracles, making them my miracles. It was truly a personal and intentional choice, and not one influenced by anything else.

During my times of contemplation and questioning, I came to the belief that if I were to forsake spirituality and religion entirely, I would lose the miracles in my life. I couldn't imagine a life without them. They truly reinforce and support my decisions and serve as a tangible reminder that I am on the correct path in life. I don't know how else to define or explain it, which I see as a good thing actually. My decision was so clear and simple to make for myself that it really didn't need any more defining or explaining of any kind. Once a permanent, life-assuring decision has been made with great conviction, as I had, the rest is made simple. The rest is inconsequential to anyone or anything, other than to myself.

Although I grew up in a denominational religion which I have accepted in my life and of which I continue to be a member, I don't consider myself a practicing member of that particular religion. That decision, which I also intentionally made, is not because I disagree nor have anything against my religion. Although technically, I guess I do have one minor disagreement, which I will explain. That disagreement, or incongruence let's call it, isn't exclusive to my religion. That decision really applies to every religion out there. In essence, I do not view my decision as being against my religion per se, because it applies to all of them.

Here is what I'm talking about. Ever since I can remember, I have always had a very deep and personal belief and connection to a higher being, such as God. The key word in that preceding sentence is "personal". For me, it has always been a deeply personal and private faith and belief, almost to the point where I did not want to share nor felt comfortable sharing it with others. Consequently, while I personally practice my faith in a private setting, such as praying for example, I do not enjoy being in a larger setting, such as a church, for example. In my mind and heart, I have reconciled that my faith is personal and private, and therefore I do not require or need to be in a church setting. Although I inconsistently attend church on occasion, I prefer not going. That's not to say that I don't enjoy the experience while I'm there either. I just prefer the experience to be in my own private setting the vast majority of the time.

While being in a church environment is completely normal for many practicing denominational members, it isn't for me. Again, it is simply because I prefer to practice my faith alone and in private. Over the years, I developed my own idea of a definition of this decision, what I came to call the "unchurch". It is basically my version of not requiring a church environment to practice my faith. In other words, I never felt that a building with other congregational members and a revered clergyman conducting the ceremony was necessary. I certainly don't have anything against churches or any other venerable building of other religions. I just prefer my "unchurch" perspective of handling my own affairs of my faith and religion. I truly feel more connected with a higher faith in the unchurch scenario than I do when I'm physically in a church.

Additionally, while it's also very normal for many practicing members to share their experiences and "recruit" and/or proselytize in the general sense, that's also not for me. I have never felt that sharing my personal faith and religion was ever the proper course of action to impose on any other human. Because religion is one area of our lives that is mostly entirely based on faith, I never believed that convincing someone else to have the same belief as mine was respectful to that other person, who has his own free will. Although this seems a bit ironic in that you are reading my book about helping you become a better person, there is one massively significant difference. Convincing/converting someone of your religion inherently entails the understanding that you now have to believe in a higher being, which takes the primary focus away from the self first. I believe that the self comes first and that the higher being serves as a spiritual guide of a righteous path. My book is 100% devoted to the self and nothing more. In fact, I've already prefaced this section by saying that it does not have to be viewed as a necessary step in your transcendence of the self. It is clearly and most definitely your choice as to how you view spirituality and religion and whether or not it has a place in your life.

Another important reason why I believe it is disingenuous to impose someone's faith on another is precisely because it primarily revolves around faith. Faith is a mostly intangible (many would say completely intangible) state of being that requires someone to choose to believe, which is very difficult to do. Choosing to believe in something is and should be a difficult process. It is not a quick decision by any means. You're not deciding what to eat off a menu. Choice and choosing can be a very long contemplative endeavor that is most private to a person. For a person to choose to believe, that person would have to go through a very long, internalized analysis of oneself to even have a glimmer of hope that they are able to come to a definitive decision. I realize that for many people, perhaps most people, they were born into a religion, so they had a default acceptance of it from a young age. There's not much pondering required there. But trying to convince or convert someone to your faith from another faith or perhaps from no faith is a totally different matter of great significance, delicacy, and respect.

One of the reasons why I personally chose to believe in my spirituality and my religion is because I saw miracles as tangible, credible evidence for myself. In other words, my faith is not 100% based on the pure belief of it. For me, the belief in my faith is bolstered by what I view as tangible miracles in my life. My point is that having some form of tangible reference and guidance is important and helpful in literally any and every decision-making process. Therefore, for me, my faith is grounded in substance. My faith is also grounded by my chosen ways of practicing my belief in a personal and private manner, which is borne of nothing less than my strong conviction in that choice. There is no shame, regret, or doubt in that choice.

On the subject of an afterlife of some form, I've also come to believe in its existence, a decision that was also made after great contemplation and analysis. It occurred to me that although there is nothing tangible in the way of proof or irrefutable evidence proving an afterlife's existence, I forced myself to try to arrive at a realization that to me would be the closest tangible evidence of a possible afterlife. I truly believe I have done so. While this is still only my personal opinion, one that can be debated or rejected, I have complete conviction in this realization, which I would be willing to debate with anyone at any time. For me, I have convinced myself that there has to be an afterlife. While I cannot speak to the type of afterlife, I believe that at a bare minimum, ours souls do continue to live on in some form, and that we will maintain consciousness of that form. This realization and conviction, in turn, re-affirmed and bolstered my belief that there has to be a spiritual higher power that has created such an afterlife.

After tremendous amount of contemplation in my younger years, I remember finally having a moment of clarity on this subject in my twenties. My initial focus became what the opposite of an afterlife would be. In other words, the opposite of afterlife would be death in its simplest and purest form, meaning that the moment we die, it instantly becomes a complete, irreversible lights-out. This would literally be in its most final form where there is absolutely zero possibility of having any remote sense of consciousness, even on the most miniscule level. Let's assume this to be the case, that there is zero chance of consciousness, therefore zero chance of an afterlife. Let's assume that death is the ultimate form of complete blackness, the darkest and blackest black you can ever conjure up. This train of thinking brought me to the final way that I can describe it, which is the state of nothingness. Death would be the ultimate state of nothingness.

If the state of nothingness is where we go upon death, then let's try to imagine a state of nothingness. Let's see if we can conceptualize nothingness, if we can even think of what nothingness feels like. I think we can all agree that the closest measurement we have to nothingness/death is when we sleep, but even then we are not dead. Our brain, among all other biological life functions, is still 100% alive and active. Therefore, sleep is not a good example to use when contemplating a state of nothingness. The only other remaining option is to try to force our minds to literally think of nothingness, to try to conceptualize the state of nothingness. I have desperately tried to conjure up in my brain what nothingness feels like, or could feel like, or even come close to grasping some sort of notion of nothingness. No matter how hard I tried with every attempt throughout my life, I've never ever been able to literally think or conceptualize a state of nothingness, nor could I explain it to myself in any sensible manner. I got nothing (bad pun alert) out of my failed attempts of trying to grasp nothingness. It was literally impossible. I couldn't do it. Every time I tried, I drove myself nuts trying to harness all the power of my mind to get there.

I thus came to the realization that the human mind cannot grasp even the notion of nothingness. Because of this reality, I came to the realization that if I can't conceive the state of nothing, then there has to be something beyond nothing, beyond death. To me, this was as close to tangible proof that our soul is immortal because it does not allow us to conceive its mortality in a nothingness state. In other words, our soul cannot die if I can't even grasp any sense of a notion of such a death. I therefore believed that if we are not able to rationalize a state of nothingness, then that leaves the door open that there must be some sort of afterlife where our souls live on. If our souls are immortal, then an afterlife has to exist for our souls to have a path of immortal continuance. This is how and why I have a belief in an afterlife in which my soul continues in some fashion.

I urge you to try for yourself. Go ahead, take an hour, a day, a year, a lifetime, if needed, to see if you can conceptualize and explain to me a state of nothingness. Try to harness the power of your mind in the best way you are capable and see if you can come to a real clarity on the state of nothingness. Now I realize that the obvious argument against my hypothesis is that maybe the human mind is simply not capable of grasping a state of nothingness. I thought of that also. However, I truly believe that our minds are tremendously powerful, more than we can ever know. I wouldn't have written on this very topic as one of my central themes of this book if I didn't believe that. I therefore have no doubt that our minds are capable of this most difficult comprehension of nothingness, if it is possible. The fact that it isn't possible, or at least it wasn't for me, formed my opinion on the matter. If you're able to achieve this seemingly impossible challenge, I'd love to hear from you. Maybe your experience and ultimate achievement might disabuse me of my position on the afterlife.

Allow me to share another direct personal story in my life that served as additional form of evidentiary proof of an afterlife for me. I had the privilege and the most indescribable angelic moment of being with my mother when she took her last breath. It was both the saddest day of my life and the most life-assuring one as well. This was the only time in my life that I was able to witness a life come to an end right in front of me, a moment and experience like no other and one I will certainly never forget. It was such an other-worldly and indescribable experience that is difficult to explain on any level. I will certainly share with you the best I can.

Most peoples' experiences with the death of a loved one are usually where they are informed of the death after the fact. In other words, most people do not have the unique experience of witnessing and being in the presence of the actual moment of when death comes to a person. It is certainly not an experience that is in anyone's control. This is one of the many moments in life where situations simply happen and/or present themselves to you. In my case, I was very fortunate and felt extremely blessed and privileged to have experienced the most unique, life-affirming moment by being with her. Witnessing life affirmation during a moment of one's death is both ironic and indescribably incredible. Additionally, the ironic symbolism of my mother birthing my life and me being there for the last moment of her life was certainly not lost on me.

At this juncture, my mother was in the latter stage of cancer, in a nursing home. Her weight had been steadily dropping on a daily basis to its final sixty-two pounds. Her normal weight was about 115 pounds. When she dropped to about 100, I became fearfully concerned that she might be at the end stage of life. After her weight fell below eighty pounds, I told myself that the end could be any day now. Every day I would be with her at the nursing home, and every day I felt that the final day was sadly nearing. She graciously surprised me by living several weeks longer than I had imagined. In hindsight, I really believe she was stubbornly holding on to life just for me. I'd like to think that she did it for me because I insistently and selfishly kept begging her to hold on a little longer during every visit with her. I was so afraid to let her go that I literally kept begging her not to die, thinking of only of myself. She was incredibly lucid and clear-headed all the way to the end, so she saw and heard every tear-filled, red-eyed plea for life I made to her. She was fully aware of every moment we spent together and every single moment was incredibly precious. I truly felt and lived the fragile preciousness of life in those final moments.

When her weight dropped into the sixties, I became indescribably terrified of her imminent death. I can't even describe the contradictory feeling of knowing that a loved one is dying yet still hoping that it doesn't actually happen. On what was to be her final day, I got a phone call from her nurse before noon telling me to come see her as soon as possible (I would usually visit her in the afternoon). Nurses have been witness to death many times, so they know when it's coming. The call freaked me the hell out. I don't even remember how I suddenly appeared in my mother's room, as if I was teleported. I sat next to her as always, as she lay there. She was so happy to see me. She had waited for me. We talked briefly. She asked me to move her a bit and adjust the blankets to make her more comfortable. As soon as I made her more comfortable, she started to go.

I selfishly begged her again to hold on, but this time, she was ready. I could see it in her face. She was at peace. All she wanted was to see me for the last time and for me to make her comfortable. At this very moment, I saw the biggest miracle I had ever seen in my life. I literally saw her life physically drain away from her face. It looked and felt as if the most ethereal mist was leaving her face in that very moment. I'd like to think it was her soul. I believe I may have seen my mother's soul leaving her body. One moment her face was full of life and the next it turned hollow and flat.

When the nurse came in to take her pulse, there was still a faint pulse that lasted for about another five minutes. I felt it myself. The nurse indicated that it's normal for that to occur. If that's normal, for the heart to continue beating for a few minutes, then why was there the appearance of death on her face, why was there the visual of life leaving her, which I witnessed? I'd like to believe that it was because her soul was leaving the physical body. Whatever chemical reactions continued to take place in her physical body after that, they did so without her soul in it.

I will never forget this amazing blessing of a moment that the universe allowed me to share with my mother. I had been completely terrified of the thought of my mother passing and of the unknown upon her passing. But once I shared those actual last few moments with her, they were the most majestic, peaceful and awe-inspiring LIFE moments I could ever spend with someone. The fear and terror of death completely disappeared from me. What was there was the beauty and preciousness of her life that I shared with her. I saw that she was happy, at peace, and completely ready to move on, her soul that is. I really believe that she was at peace *because* she could see she was moving on right before it happened. She had no doubt in her facial expressions. As soon as I made her comfortable and told her I loved her for the last time, it was as if a door had opened in her mind that she knew she must step through. I witnessed her life in her body one moment, then in the next, I was witness to her immortal soul moving on to another life form of some kind. It was incredibly transformational for me and still indescribable to this day.

You may have gathered by now that I'm more of a spiritual person than a congregational-practicing religious person. I would say that is a fair statement. While I do greatly believe and have faith in a higher being (such as God), I also believe and am awed by the incredible and indescribable forces of spirituality, the universe, the cosmos, and the everyday energy-fueled human connections. I feel and see all of these things in many aspects of our lives. I've seen many instances of the universe aligning with my life in ways that create meanings, awareness, and guidance in my life. There have been countless times that the incredible chemistry of human connection has been on display. During these moments, I've felt the tangible waves of energy that come from a heightened awareness when living in the moment. In the art world alone, for example, we are constantly awed by the many instances of beauty, synchronicity, and chemistry that an artist or an ensemble of artists have magically woven together. This alone is a magical symbol of the mysteries of precious life.

In art, we routinely bear witness to a perfectly crafted song, movie, painting, sculpture, musical group, ancient and modern architecture, etc. Every single time we notice such unique magnificence, we all agree on one thing, that it is perfect. Our reaction to it is always one where it can never be summed up better than by its perfection. This is the great ironic beauty of life. While perfection for an individual is impossible, the many instances of perfection in art created by humans individually and collectively are examples and reminders that there is an incredible sense of human energy that allows for timeless creations — perfection created by imperfect humans. The artistic common bond among us can transcend into perfect creations when coming together. This is the only instance in life where imperfect beings can (1) create perfect renderings and (2) thus become immortal through those renderings.

This is why it is so unfortunate that many of us do not accept each other in the most damaging and unthinkable ways. This is the daily occurrence in the same world where alongside the destruction and devastation, there are kind people and artists who have shown with crystal clarity that coming together, accepting each other, and bearing the delicious fruit of this harmony are not only possible, but currently exist within many of us.

I believe and have hope that the ratio of human harmony over human destruction will eventually become the predominant numerator of humanity. It has to. The better part of humanity will prevail because our very survival depends on it. I believe in the math that although human discord still represents a large portion that only seems to be growing, more and more people will come to the ultimate realization that all humans will have to unite to face the same common threats that are unwittingly borne of advanced technologies and accumulated devastating effects on Earth's nature.

We will eventually be forced to replace our *hatred* of one another for *acceptance* of one another, in the name of the sole remaining sake of our very survival. This ultimate global human union, the likes of which have never occurred in mankind's history to this point, will become the prevailing norm after mankind survives and overcomes today's forces of human destruction. Human harmony will then continue to endure because all of us will have been witness to the global acceptance that our formidable unity is the only way to ensure humanity's continued survival. We will all finally come to know the simple human truth that the hatred of our past no longer has a place in the future of our collective lives, a future where everyone is seen as a friend and neighbor.

"We are not human beings having a spiritual experience; we are spiritual beings having a human experience."

PIERRE TEILHARD DE CHARDIN

"The unexamined life is not worth living."

SOCRATES

FINAL STAGE 19: BLAST OFF!!!:

You've Come to Life!

It's time to blast off into the new you! This is the most important Stage in your journey to Live in the REAL! This is the final *ACTION* stage. Nothing is ever accomplished without action. Making life-altering decisions in your mind is the first step, but without a commitment to converting these decisions to actionable changes, everything remains theoretical in your life. You don't want to live a theoretical life, you want to live an actionable life, a life of consistent, forward-moving action. The goal is not theory, the goal is practical action. How often do you see your friends talking about their hopes, dreams, and changes they want to make, but not having the courage to do so? Quite often, I would imagine.

If you haven't done so already to this point, then now (this moment) is when you have to make a committed decision to begin living your authentic self in your REAL life. The title of this Stage, "You've Come to Life" carries all of the following meanings for you. It means (1) that you have finally arrived at your true life, (2) that your life has opened up for you in ways you never imagined, (3) that you have a greater awareness and appreciation for all of life in general, and (4) that this is a second birth for you, a re-birth if you will.

In my lifetime, I've made many life-changing actionable decisions. I've changed long-term careers, I've forsaken or not pursued other careers, and I've taken the roads less traveled by. These are just the major life-altering markers of my life. I've also consistently made several less major decisions in my life in the constant pursuit of becoming a better person and living my authentic REAL identity. Consequently, I personally have come to life many times, and I will continue to do so in this continuing, majestic journey of life.

Here is the most important way for you to truly achieve not only a changed mental and heartfelt perspective of your life, but to really start living it. Remember in the Forward of my book regarding the very first thing that I highlighted? It was that I'm not here to motivate you, I'm here to eternally inspire you. I'm not a motivator, I'm an Inspirer. Motivation, as you may recall, is dependent on a consistent external stimulus, so it's therefore short-term and temporary. Inspiration comes from within. Inspiration is an inward choice you make that permanently changes your perspective on any matter. It's the ultimate self-help way of living with your permanent changes. Inspiration *is* self-help at its core. Being inspired ignites self-help into action.

My message of action is simple. Take what you've been inspired by in this book and make it permanent. Fully commit to it as I've outlined within every Stage, and take the baby steps on a gradual, daily basis to effect little changes in your life. These little changes will snowball into an avalanche of a new life for you, before you know it. It's a constant, life-long process. Starting is the most important actionable part.

I genuinely hope that I was able to "teach you how to fish" and that you're now able to easily catch as many fish as you'd like in the pursuit of your new life's satiation. This new avalanche of life will become the building blocks of your ultimate and immortal legacy. Think about the everlasting legacy you want to create and leave for others. Visualize it, frame it in your mind, and live in it ever day! You have the power to effect and manifest it. Now go do it! Live in pursuit of your future legacy as your REAL self. Once you start on this path, you won't want to stop. Toss this book aside and *Live in the REAL!* REAL is rare. Let's make it normal together.

BULLET SUMMARIES OF THE MAJOR CONCLUDING THEMES:

- *On Life:* The preciousness of life is the most sacred. Understanding your life starts with appreciating the preciousness of yours and the greater life of humanity. A heart never stops beating to give you life, so don't live your life in ways to give your heart a reason to stop.

- *On Truth:* Truths are self-evident and are easily seen, without effort any longer, when you are living in the REAL. They are self-revealing and exist in front of you in your everyday life. You are no longer a truth *seeker*, you're a truth *seer*. Seeking truth is no longer the process because you have internally created a programmed mind of truth *seeing* not seeking. Living in the philosophy of REALogy® based on truth has become a core template of your life.

- *On Time:* Time ticks away literally every second. You can never re-capture any lost moment in time. Spend it wisely for it occurs with or without your appreciation. Do not kill time, as the old and sad cliché goes. Live time, and live in time…every moment of it.

- *On Change:* Change also occurs with or without you. Why then are you always fighting it? Change is a constant. Drop your fears and go with change, not against it. Become one within the flow of change, like catching and riding the perfect wave.

- *On Mind:* The power of your mind has no limit of its potency. Whenever you have doubt of any kind, lean on that power first. Remember that by harnessing our mind's power, anything is achievable. Achieving a committed decision of change first starts in your mind, a decision that becomes the engine that activates your wheels to motion.

- *On Fear:* An important way to view any type of fear you might have going forward in your life is to completely eliminate the word "fear" from you vocabulary and mind. Permanently change your mind's paradigm of fear altogether. Instead of the word "fear", permanently replace it with the word "concern". This way, there are no more fears to face, just mere concerns. Concerns are much more manageable because they inherently mean that any given situation is simply a matter of questioning and addressing a situation, with a goal of resolution and overcoming it. Instead of being crippled in a situation by fear, viewing it as a concern merely makes it a task that you have to complete. "Concern" makes it tangible and therefore addressable. "Fear" makes it unknown and therefore anxiety-inducing. Changing your perspective in this way automatically and psychologically calms you and places you in a comfortable mental state of tackling the problem instead of avoiding or delaying it.

- *On Your History:* While your history, personal tragedies, and/or your horrible childhood environment may have caused traumas and paralysis that have prevented you from moving forward in life, they cannot be used as excuses. Once they are brought to light, understood, and reconciled, your commitment to resolve them and forge ahead is yours alone. You have the ability and power to transcend your personal history and make the necessary changes to forsake that history and start anew. Breaking your chains and ending that cycle is in your grasp.

- *On Health:* Health and fitness have morphed into an additional appendage on your body that you cannot do without. If you stop breathing, you die. If you stop living a daily lifestyle centered on your optimal health, then you will die much sooner than your lifelong potential. Why allow that in your life when it's 100% avoidable by a simple choice of commitment?

- *On Life Fitness:* Your mindset of life fitness comprises the daily goals of completed life enhancements, which further improve your life fitness. Accomplishing these self-monitored tasks and goals on a daily basis will make you a better person each and every day, thereby enhancing and improving upon the fitness of your life. This daily routine will become an ingrained and effortless facet of your life that now aligns your sense of purpose, meaning, and growth on the same path of continued achievements. This cycle continues to enhance your life fitness.

- *On Relationships:* Your relationships are the life-blood of your life. They keep the blood pumping. You have to nurture and protect them. Without your relationships, your support system suffers. We all need love and encouragement. It's difficult to manage life without your support system. The most important relationship is the one with your true self.

- *On Identity:* Do not define your real identity with the potentially false one tied to your position or career. Life doesn't work that way. While it's fine to have passion and be passionate about your career, which you should, the total definition of your identity shouldn't be solely based on it.

- *On Money:* Money, materialism, addictions, need I say more? Your warped and skewed view of what they mean in your life will be the ultimate downfall of your life, one that typically becomes a lonely one.

- *On Love from the Heart:* You have to completely destroy the antiquated survival-based default mechanism that humans had long ago. Everyday life is not about living in fear and viewing others as the enemy. Your default mechanism should be centered on love and your heart. Life is about loving and accepting others. Remove any and all hate from your core existence as hate is a slow killer of oneself.

- *On Meaning:* There's no such thing as the meaning of life. There are many, unlimited meanings of life. Life is about your personal journey of finding as many meanings as possible for yourself, to therefore live your most authentic life.

- *On Miracles:* View the reasons of why things happen to you as miracles. When you fully understand these everyday miracles, you will grasp the reasons of why things happen to you, leading to the realizations of the ultimate meanings in your life.

- *On Roles:* Why must there be a debate about how different men and women are and which is the better gender? Makes no sense to me whatsoever. We are all the same! I can't make it any clearer than that, other than to say that we must all have an unadulterated, equal-footed respect for one another.

- *On Words:* Words are the most powerful means of our human communication. This is a two-edged sword. We should be using it for clear, respectful discourse and communication, not for squashing another person's humanity into the ground.

- *On Growth:* What is your life without any personal growth? How is it possible to live a life without any bettering of oneself? I guess it's possible. But it shouldn't be so. If you agree, then your time for unlimited growth starts now.

- *On the World:* If you think living in our world is hard, see what happens when your live it as the REAL self-actualized you. Actually, it becomes oh so much easier. You're able to live your life without any limitations and impositions in the current world any longer. You're finally free. Living your REAL life is now made easy.

- *On Faith:* Having spirituality and/or religion in your life is a personal choice. While a true authentic REAL life can be achieved without it, life itself doesn't judge or place any limitations on your free will nor how you use it.

- *On the New You:* You've finally come to life! At this point, simply stated, do what you really want! When you do this, the path to wisdom is clearer and shorter. Just don't hurt anyone in the process. In fact, try to love, help, and share with others along your journey. Leave an eternal legacy for the world of which you can be proud.

- *On Your New Perspective:* On your new life's journey, don't forget to approach every situation as a kid, with a child's innocence, exuberance, imagination, and hopefulness. The game of life can be and should be fun. Any time you feel a setback of sorts, just remember that you're a kid at heart. So just have fun!

LIVE IN THE REAL!
REAL is rare. Let's make it normal.